OLDHAM

CORPORATION

BUSES

By

David Wayman

First published 1997

ISBN   1 900515 05 9

Published by DTS Publishing Limited
PO Box 105, Croydon, Surrey

Printed by Staples Printers (Rochester) Limited

© David Wayman 1997

British Library Cataloguing in Publication Data. A catalogue record for this book is available from the British Library.

FRONT COVER: A sunny Mumps Bridge sees 1957 Roe-bodied Leyland PD2/20 No 405 on yet another journey from Derker to Royton (Stottfield) on service 11 in the 1960s. *(Photobus—Roy Marshall)*

TITLE PAGE: Oldham No 368 was one of four 1950-built Crossley-bodied Crossley DD42/8s and has most fortunately been preserved. 368 is seen here in the ownership of Crossley Omnibus Society at Stalybridge whilst on a private tour. The impressive lines of the Crossley bodywork give the bus a very substantial appearance, further enhanced by the impressive Crossley radiator. *(Ian N. Lynas)*

BELOW: Seen at the top of Yorkshire Street on its way to taking up a journey on service 8 (Hollinwood – Shaw) is 330, a 1949 Daimler CVD6 with Crossley body that may be compared with that make of bodywork on a Crossley chassis as shown in the picture of 307 on page 45. Daimler 330 was one of six to receive a chromium-plated radiator shell and engine from withdrawn Birmingham Corporation buses acquired for spare parts in 1964. The Crossley bodies did not have an upper saloon crimson lake band when new but 330 received one during a subsequent repaint when the lining-out was omitted. Among the vehicles following are another Daimler bus and a Triumph Herald Car. *(J. Fozard)*

High Street, Oldham

OLDHAM BEFORE BUS DAYS—Two commercial postcards. Above: Oldham High Street and below: Union Street. *(Both author's collection)*

Union Street, Oldham

OLDHAM
CORPORATION BUSES

CONTENTS

OLDHAM IN THE 1980s: Only three months before bus deregulation in October 1986 and working the service that was previously No 12, Greater manchester PTE's Northern Counties-bodied Leyland Olympian 3041 (B41 PJA), a successor to Oldham Corporation buses, stops in the pedestrianised High Street to do what buses are meant to do. *(Author)*

Acknowledgements

I wish to express grateful thanks to those mentioned below for their kind co-operation and ready assistance with the various aspects of the preparation and writing of this book.

R Atkinson, the late A. Blomley, C. Carter, T. B. Collinge, the late R. Dunning, J. Fletcher, J. Fozard, P. Fox (Oldham Leisure Services), Greater Manchester Museum of Transport, the late J. Hall, J. Hartley, C. W. Heaps, G. G. Hilditch, B. A. Hill, A. Holland, J. J. Holmes, A. Howard-Smith, Manchester Transport Museum Society, R. Marshall, T. B. Maund, Oldham Evening Chronicle, E. Ogden, H. W. Peers, Mrs. E. Powell, A. Renshaw, Ribble Enthusiasts' Club, J. Senior, the late R. Taylor, A. A. Townsin, the Transport Ticket Society, E. Watts, G. Weigh, S. West, M. Wild.

DAVID WAYMAN   OLDHAM, MAY 1997

Some decimal and metric equivalents

1d (one penny)	= 0.4166p	1s 0d (one shilling, =12d)	= 5p
1 ton	= 1,016kg	7 tons	= 7,112kg
1ft	= 0.3048m	30ft	= 9.144m

"Here it comes now, look!"

"Good heavens, what a row! What a smell!"

Maybe that's what they said. Maybe a dog joined in with a sustained howl. Maybe a cat scampered up a ginnel.

Yes, perhaps that is how it happened on the winding and cobbled Union Street West between Oldham's town centre and the residential area called the Coppice. The event would have been the passing of the first Corporation motor bus on the first journey of the first bus service in town. It was on 12 May 1913 that this took place and to Oldham people it must have seemed that they could now boast the utmost in modernity so far as local transport was concerned.

To set the local scene, however, the nature of Oldham's terrain is perhaps suggested by its name which may derive from the Saxon *Auld Hulme* or *Aldholme,* denoting "an elevated situation" and "meadow land". It could be interpreted as "the meadow on the hill". The Oldham scene is dominated by hills. Much of the town centre is almost 700ft above sea level, making it about 500ft higher than central Manchester, some seven miles to the south-west. To the north-east, the gruelling climb up to the bleak Pennine moorlands reaches the 1,100ft contour less than four miles from Oldham centre. The town and its environs, therefore, comprise much challenging ground on which to run public transport. Fierce gradients make severe demands on vehicles and require above-average skills from their handlers in the best of weather. In winter, ice, snow and high winds pose greater hazards and it is a tribute to past generations of transport people that such high degrees of safety and reliability have been achieved.

Oldham, at the centre of a former coalmining, hat-making and subsequently cotton-spinning area, sits astride the principal ancient Pennine highways running from south-

This 1994 view of Oldham town centre, looking south-west, shows the Civic Centre tower block (right of centre ground) at the top of West Street, which falls steeply out of sight to the right and meets Middleton Road. Left of near-centre, the long roofs running transversely are those of the Market Hall although the spot referred to as 'Market Place' for bus and tram purposes, altitude 691ft, is now practically covered by the domed building (left of centre ground) which is part of the Spindles shopping complex. Left of the grassed area (far centre) is part of Union Street West which was on Oldham's first bus route to the Coppice (beyond, centre and left). Running out of the picture diagonally (right middle background) is Manchester Street, now dual carriageway, while the trees (centre background) are in Werneth Park. In the far background and at much lower altitudes are Hollinwood (left), Werneth (centre) and Chadderton (right). *(Oldham Evening Chronicle)*

west to north-east, connecting Manchester with Huddersfield, Leeds, Halifax and Bradford. Nowadays, most of the through traffic uses the M62 motorway just a few miles to the north, slicing between Oldham and neighbouring Rochdale. In bygone years, heavy convoys threaded the town's roads, impeding the local transport. A further important road passes through Oldham centrally from north to south, linking Rochdale and Ashton-under-Lyne. Cotton mills and engineering works became well-established in Oldham from the 19th century and the adjacent Urban Districts of Chadderton, Failsworth, Lees and Shaw and Crompton coalesced to form one urban area with Oldham as its main centre. When local government boundaries and functions were reorganised in 1974, along with the more dispersed Saddleworth Urban District Council in the West Riding of Yorkshire, the smaller authorities were to combine with Oldham County Borough to form Oldham Metropolitan District (or Borough) in the Greater Manchester Metropolitan Area (or County).

A branch railway from Middleton to Oldham was opened on 31 March 1842 and, by 1863, there were rail links with all the neighbouring towns. Surprisingly, the direct line to Manchester via Failsworth was not completed until 17 May 1880. Population trends in the late Victorian era brought demands for a more local transport system. The Manchester Carriage Co developed a large network of horse-drawn tramways and sought to establish lines in Oldham. Wisely, the Town Council decided to lay the tracks itself and lease them to the company. Cars started running between Waterhead and Hollinwood on 1 November 1880, the Hollinwood–Manchester link opening on 28 March 1881. The steep gradients and the need for special types of car caused the Waterhead–Hollinwood section to be worked separately in horse-tram days.

Oldham Council made a similar decision with a Royton–Hathershaw tramway line which was leased to the Manchester, Bury, Rochdale and Oldham Steam Tramways Co. This concern had a gauge of 3ft 6in north of Royton but the Council insisted on the standard measure of 4ft 8½in on the lines it laid itself to conform with the existing Waterhead–Manchester line. This resulted in the MBR&O's depot at Royton having two entrances, one with 3ft 6in gauge rails and the other with standard gauge. The steam tramway was worked by four-wheel condensing locomotives hauling double-deck trailers and commenced operations between Royton and Hathershaw on 1 August 1885 and from Royton on to a branch along Featherstall Road to serve Platt's works near Werneth station on 4 July 1889. With a few horse-drawn buses on secondary routes this network served the area until the turn of the century when that technological marvel, the electric tramcar, revolutionised public transport.

The electric tramway

ABOVE: The well-supported ceremonial occasion in Park Road depicted here, possibly the opening of the tramway there on 15 June 1901, illustrates the normal layout of double deck trams early in the 20th century. The vehicle is car 3 which has double bogies but was later rebuilt with top cover and a four-wheel single truck. *(J. J. Holmes collection)*

Oldham Corporation, like so many of the larger local authorities, opted to run its own tramways and also took on the responsibility for those of neighbouring Royton, Crompton and Lees, exercising powers enshrined in the Oldham Corporation Act, 1899. Lines were laid along all the main thorougfares and to Glodwick and Hollins. At Hathershaw, the Oldham tracks met those of a British Electric Traction Group subsidiary company, the Oldham, Ashton and Hyde Electric Tramway Limited, but there was no through running until 1921. Oldham met Rochdale Corporation tracks at Royton Summit (Thornham) and a joint service from Hathershaw through to Rochdale and beyond ran from 1 May 1906 for seven years. Hollinwood was the meeting place of Oldham and Manchester Corporation tramways and through running was to last from 1907 to the end of Oldham's system and was then carried on with buses. At the

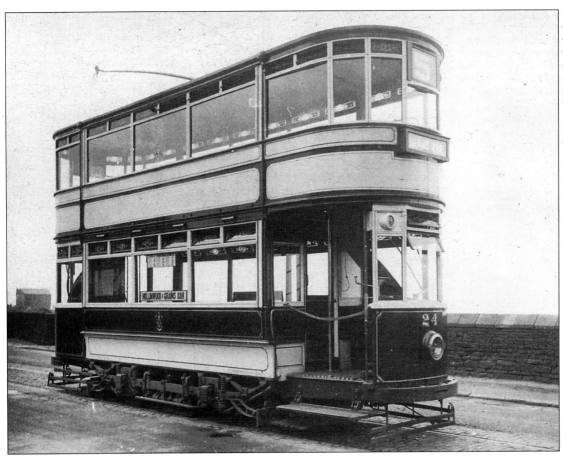

Free Trade Inn, near the Oldham County Borough/Chadderton Urban District boundary on Middleton Road, the Corporation tracks met those of the Middleton Electric Traction Company, through running commencing in 1925.

At its peak in 1927, the Oldham Corporation tram fleet totalled 122 cars of which 112 were double-deckers with up to 60 seats.

Oldham's electric tram services developed during the first two years as follows, although some horse and steam trams continued running until 31 October 1901 and 28 June 1902 respectively.

15 Dec 00	Middleton Road (Chadderton boundary)–West Street/ Rochdale Road
15 Jun 01	Cross St–Lees Rd (Lees boundary)
15 Jun 01	Lees Rd–Glodwick Rd–Ashton Rd
18 Jul 01	Ashton Rd (Junction Hotel)–Hollins Rd (Crown & Mitre)
29 Aug 01	Ashton Rd–Hollins Rd–extended from Crown & Mitre to Hollinwood
7 Mar 02	Hollinwood–Ashton Rd–extended to Star Inn
19 Apr 02	Middleton Rd–West St/Rochdale Rd–extended to Hollins Rd via Star Inn
1 May 02	Star Inn–Ashton Rd–Hathershaw
17 May 02	Hollinwood–Werneth–Waterhead
22 May 02	Lees Rd–Glodwick Rd–Park Rd–Ashton Rd–extended to form circular service via Union St
22 May 02	Lees Rd (Lees boundary)–Cross St–extended to Market Pl
9 Jun 02	Lees Rd (Lees boundary)–Market Pl–extended to Hollinwood via Hollins
9 Jun 02	Middleton Rd linked with Hathershaw instead of Hollins Rd
30 Aug 02	Middleton Rd linked with Shaw Rd–Higginshaw instead of Hathershaw
30 Aug 02	Hathershaw linked with Boundary Park instead of Middleton Rd
4 Sept 02	Higginshaw–Egerton St–Rock St/Lord St (branch line from Shaw Rd)

18 Oct 02	Lees Rd (Lees boundary) linked with Market Pl–Henshaw St–Chadderton Rd instead of Hollinwood
18 Oct 02	Hollinwood–Hollins linked with Hill Stores instead of Lees Rd (Lees boundary)
18 Oct 02	Market Pl–Moorside
19 Nov 02	Werneth Fire Stn–Featherstall Rd–Boundary Pk
11 Dec 02	Middleton Rd linked with Wellington St instead of Higginshaw
11 Dec 02	Higginshaw linked with Union St W instead of Middleton Rd

As will be seen there were numerous alterations and extensions to the pattern during the first few years, some of them short-lived but, on 25 March 1903, the network was as summarised below.

Waterhead–Werneth–Hollinwood
Hollinwood–Hollins Rd–Union St–Watersheddings
Lees Rd (Lees boundary)–Werneth Fire Stn
Higginshaw–Mumps–Union St W
Werneth Fire Stn–Featherstall Rd–Boundary Pk
Middleton Rd (Chadderton boundary)–Wellington St
Hathershaw–Star Inn–Boundary Pk
Market Pl–Watersheddings–Moorside
Circular (Union St–Glodwick Rd–Park Rd–Star Inn)
Higginshaw–Egerton St–Rock St/Lord St
Market Pl–Henshaw St–Chadderton Rd

Further significant or long-standing developments took place on the dates mentioned here:

1 Aug 03	Lees Rd line extended to Lees (County End)
5 Nov 04	Hathershaw–Boundary Park service extended to Summit
15 Nov 04	Market Pl–Higginshaw service extended to Shaw (Wren's Nest)
13 Apr 05	Werneth Fire Stn–Boundary Pk service extended to Shaw (Beal Lane) via Royton
1 May 06	Hathershaw–Summit service extended through Rochdale to Norden (joint with Rochdale Corporation), discontinued 1913 as those of Oldham's cars that were being top-covered were too high to pass under a bridge in Rochdale

21 Jan 07	Waterhead–Werneth–Hollinwood service extended to Manchester (Stevenson Sq, later Piccadilly, later Stevenson Sq) via Failsworth, Newton Heath, Miles Platting (joint with Manchester Corporation)
14 Sep 12	Egerton St–Rock St/Lord St line closed
4 Jun 14	Moorside line extended to Grains Bar
1 Dec 19	Werneth Fire Stn–Shaw (Beal Lane) extended to Shaw (Wren's Nest)
31 Jan 21	Shaw (Wren's Nest)–Werneth Fire Stn extended to Hollinwood
2 Jul 21	Star Inn–Ashton through service commenced (joint with Ashton-under-Lyne Corporation)
9 Aug 25	Market Pl–Middleton Rd (Chadderton boundary) service extended following purchase of Chadderton boundary–Mills Hill line from Middleton Electric Traction Company, with through running continuing over Mills Hill–Middleton section purchased (with other lines) from MET Co by Middleton Borough Council and leased to Manchester Corporation. New service then: Oldham (Market Pl)–Middleton

TRAM ROUTE NUMBERING

The following tram service numbers were applied in March 1921

1	Waterhead–Werneth–Hollinwood
2	Lees–Werneth–Hollinwood
3	Market Pl–Middleton Rd
4	Circular
5	Grains Bar–Moorside–Hollins–Hollinwood
6	Moorside–Hollins–Hollinwood
7	Hathershaw–Star Inn–Summit
8	Shaw (Wren's Nest)–Featherstall Rd–Werneth–Hollinwood
9	Shaw (Wren's Nest)–Higginshaw–Mumps–Market Pl–Chadderton Rd
10	Union St W–Mumps–Waterhead
11	High St–Werneth–Hollinwood
12	Star Inn–Market Pl–Watersheddings
14	Star Inn–Hathershaw–Ashton (from 2 Jul 21, joint with Ashton-under-Lyne Corporation)
20	Waterhead–Werneth–Hollinwood–Manchester (joint with Manchester Corporation)

NOTE: There is some inconsistency with the names used in the records for some termini and intermediate points. For clarity, they have been standardised in the summaries.

Particulars of the gradual abandonment of the tramway system are given with those of the replacment bus services.

B

PRIMITIVE TIMES

So there had been buses and trams drawn by horses, then steam trams followed by electric trams which in 1913 still had another 33 years to run. Next, in order to create a link where there was none, a motor bus service was started between the Town Hall and the Coppice, almost a mile away to the south-west, on weekdays only. Powers to run motor buses had been enshrined in the Oldham Corporation Act, 1909. Operation was restricted to the County Borough of Oldham and the term "motor omnibus" included those powered by steam or electricity. Later, the Oldham Corporation Act, 1925, would extend bus-operating powers to include any district outside the town boundary, subject to the consent of the local authority concerned. This consent was not required where the route was within a five-mile radius of the Oldham boundary except for some parts of Failsworth Urban District.

The Coppice bus service first ran on 12 May 1913, as mentioned previously, and four days later a second one was commenced as a tram feeder. It was on the north-eastern side of town, running along the road that became the A672, from the Moorside tram terminus to Grains Bar just under a mile away. The outer bus terminus was at a breezy Pennine crossroad with a few houses, 1,115ft above sea level. Although the bus ran on "certain days" only,

apparently weekdays, the General Manager was authorised by the Tramways Committee to run it during summer weekends at his discretion as the Grains Bar area was popular for picnics and country walks. The introduction of the bus service was a temporary measure pending the extension of the tram tracks to Grains Bar. Trams began running to that spot, the highest tram terminus in Britain, from 4 June 1914. The bus service was then withdrawn but a another feeder was introduced on 31 August, running north for 1° miles from the exposed Grains Bar summit to Denshaw village, sheltering in a vale and until the 1974 reorganisation of boundaries, part of Saddleworth Urban District in the West Riding of Yorkshire.

Two buses had been acquired for the services. They were Tilling-Stevens type TTA2 petrol-electric vehicles with the chassis-builder's own design of bodywork, possibly built by a sub-contractor, with 18 wooden garden seats on the uncovered upper deck and inward-facing wooden benches, each seating eight persons, along each side in the lower saloon. The rear platform and staircase were open to the elements and of course the tyres were solid and gave a rough ride on the granite setts so common in those days. A four-cylinder petrol engine with a swept volume of 3.464 litres and a rating of 40hp drove a dynamo which generated

BELOW: Oldham's first two buses, Tilling-Stevens TTA2 models with petrol-electric transmission, BU 401/402, pictured with their crews and carrying Moorside–Grains Bar route boards. *(The late R Taylor collection)*

the electricity for the motor which powered the rear axle. The need for a stepped-ratio gearbox was eliminated and the transmission system was on a similar principle to that used later in some railway locomotives. Destination and route details were carried on a board on the side of each bus and like the tramcars, buses wore a livery of crimson lake and white. They were garaged at Copsterhill Road yard, the tramways sand drier having been removed to the Glodwick yard to make room for the buses. Although they did not know it, the Corporation had made a wise choice of chassis type as the Army had no wish to commandeer petrol-electric vehicles during the Great War that was soon to commence. Petrol-electric buses, generally of Tilling-Stevens manufacture, enjoyed limited success nationally but after about 1930 could not compete with such rising

terminus of the Coppice route was altered from the Town Hall to the General Post Office in Union Street.

There was consternation on the Coppice bus one day. It had stopped at the Chamber Road/Coppice Street corner while the conductor went into a shop. A young pupil from the nearby Werneth School, James Hall, succumbed to the urge to jump on the rear platform and ring the bell twice before jumping off. The bus had gone about a hundred yards before the driver was alerted. A great to-do ensued and the headmaster was informed. Young Hall received "six o' t' best", as he recalled vividly some 75 years later, and had his name written in the punishment book. It is not known whether the conductor was disciplined by management also!

For each financial year-end during 1914-18, bus operation showed a deficit. Running costs were intolerably high,

RIGHT: The third Tilling-Stevens was BU 11, pictured here with passengers and crew at the Town Hall end of the Coppice route. (C. Carter)

stars as the Leyland Titan-Tiger and AEC Regent-Regal ranges with conventional transmission. Details of the bus fleet are given in Appendix 3.

Oldham Corporation obtained a third similar bus to provide cover for breakdowns and accidents. The County Borough of Oldham licensing authority had begun using the registration mark BU in 1907 and the first two buses were registered BU 401/402 (an explanation of the use of obliques and dashes between numbers is given in Appendix 3). During that period it was usual for void or previously used numbers to be re-issued and the third bus was BU 11. Bus services were reasonably well patronised, averaging 11 passengers per mile during the first two years. However, they gave rise to many complaints of noise, vibration, mud and high speeds (more than the 12mph limit!). The Coppice bus was re-routed more than once. The Tramways Committee actually visited the owner of one of the so-called posh houses in Wellington Road, agreeing to alter the route so that buses did not pass his front door. Moorside residents complained about the nuisance caused by the bus and by waiting passengers, a situation remedied by the extension of the tramway to Grains Bar. On 10 August 1915 the inner

the lowest being 112 per cent of receipts. Indeed, during the final six months of operation in 1919 the actual working expenses were 47.99 pence per mile—practically four shillings— a figure that was not to be reached again until 1967! Principal annual statistics are tabulated in Appendix 4. Following some serious disagreements with the Committee, the General Manager, Mr J W Dugdale, resigned on 1 March 1916 and was succeeded on 18 April by Mr Percy Priestly. A plan to sell all three buses to Rotherham Corporation came to nothing so the Committee, unable to dispose of them, sought to meet working expenses by a fares rise and service withdrawal—the Denshaw bus withdrawn on 27 August 1916, the Coppice service having been curtailed two weeks earlier due to a petrol shortage. In 1917, BU 11/402 were sold to Warrington Corporation (which re-registered them ED 1180/1181, although it is not known which became which). Coppice bus BU 401 received a second-hand single deck body and subsequently was converted to run on coal gas which was stored in a roof-mounted bag. As was to happen during the next world war, it was soon discovered that results were unsatisfactory. BU 401 was withdrawn from service and replaced by BU 69, a battery-powered vehicle acquired in February 1918 from the Electromobile Co (Leeds) Ltd, actually of Otley and builders of battery-powered vehicles during 1914-33. Buses were usually based on Commercial Truck Co chassis imported from the USA. It seems that Oldham bought only the chassis, fitting it with the single deck body from the chassis of BU 401. The bus service had to be suspended temporarily because the Ministry of Munitions had refused to sanction the delivery of the chassis *after* it had arrived in Oldham although the matter was put right within a few days. Oldham Corporation Tramways already had an Electromobile battery-powered tower wagon and were satisfied with its performance but the bus did not live up to expectations. It was unreliable and despite there being a re-charging socket in the yard of the Central Baths by the GPO terminus into which it was plugged between journeys, the Electrobus would frequently run out of "juice" before returning.

On 10 April 1918 Mr Priestly resigned to become Deputy General Manager of Liverpool Corporation Tramways. He was succeeded immediately by Mr William Chamberlain (later Sir William) who until then had held a post in Oldham Corporation Electrical Engineer's Department. He told the Tramways Committee about the situation and in view of the problems, not least the enormous costs, it was decided eventually to abandon bus operations. The original Coppice service ran for the last time on 13 September 1919 but the Electrobus could still be seen about town as it was sold to Belgrave Mills and used for staff transport between their Honeywell Lane premises and Hathershaw. They withdrew this service in August 1920 and operated services from Honeywell Lane to Star Inn and from Rhodes Bank to Chadderton (Wash Brook), using a Leyland open-top bus (TB 2554) which may have been a demonstrator. It survived to enter the Corporation fleet when bus operations were revived.

C
A FRESH START

Between 1919 and 1924, Oldham Corporation ran no buses although tram services were improved, a joint one between Oldham and Ashton-under-Lyne (four miles to the south) being introduced on 2 July 1921. Holt Bros (Rochdale) Ltd, later to become Yelloway Motor Services, inaugurated a circuitous bus service in May 1923 between Lees (County End tram terminus) and Grains Bar via Lydgate, Mossley, Uppermill, Dobcross and Delph. It was supported by Saddleworth Urban District Council *without their issuing a licence* but within a few weeks there were complaints because Holt Bros altered the service to omit Grains Bar, running as previously from Lees to Delph but then to Waterhead tram terminus via Scouthead. Grains Bar was served with a branch from Delph to Denshaw. These other short-lived services were also started:

High Crompton–New Hey;
Denshaw–New Hey; Waterhead–Denshaw;
Denshaw–Mytholmroyd (near Halifax).

In 1924 both Ribble Motor Services Ltd of Preston and the North Western Road Car Co (not the present-day com-

was eventually granted licences in Crompton Urban District where Holt's service had been irregular and from 16 October 1924 the Macclesfield-based concern ran a New Hey - Balderstone (Rochdale boundary) service. Holt's continued with irregular and unlicensed services until mid-1925 and then concentrated on operating charabancs.

Meanwhile, Oldham Corporation thought about resuming its own bus operations to serve the trams as feeders. Five single deck buses (or "saloons") were bought and garaged at the former steam tram shed in Dogford Road, Royton. Their livery, to be standard until 1930, was dark blue and white. The first new service, originally driver-only operated, began on 15 December 1924 and connected two railway stations, Mumps and Hollinwood, via the Coppice. Fuller details of the network development are given in Appendix 1.

Within three months, following objections from the London, Midland & Scottish Railway about the Hollinwood terminus being on its own private land, the service was cut back at the Hollinwood end to Chapel Road and altered at

LEFT: In 1924, as in the 1990s, Oldham passengers boarded a bus and paid the driver in accordance with the instruction seen on the cab side facing the entrance. The bus is one of the five all-Leyland C9 24-seat saloons (1-5) seen before delivery. *(Ribble Enthusiasts' Club)*

pany of that name), then of Macclesfield, tried to gain a foothold in the Oldham area. Ribble did not succeed but North Western was approved by Saddleworth which welcomed competition with Holt Bros. In March 1924, Oldham Watch Committee granted licences for a pool of 20 AEC and Daimler buses to run from Oldham (Egerton Street, near Parish Church) to Uppermill via Scouthead and Delph, and also via Lees, Grasscroft and Greenfield Station, some journeys being extended to Diggle. The service commenced on 3 April 1924 and the minimum fare of 4d within the Oldham boundary was double the tram fare. Holt Bros applied to run a similar service and when this was refused they ran illegally but ceased when faced with opposition from Oldham and Saddleworth Councils. North Western

the Mumps end to run via Greenacres Road to Greenacres. It was a heavily-graded route and the 24-seat buses were worked hard. The late Roy Taylor, a regular passenger in those days, recalled loads totalling about 75 passengers—including children—on the 1 in 9 eastbound climb of Chamber Road!

On 28 February 1925, a second service was commenced between Chadderton Road and New Moston (Broadway/Moston Lane East). This was given the identifying letter B, the Chapel Road - Greenacres service becoming A. Service B was extended at both ends on 25 July 1925 and became Royton Station - New Moston (Manchester Boundary) via Chadderton and Broadway. The letters distinguished bus services from the numbered tram services. Bus service

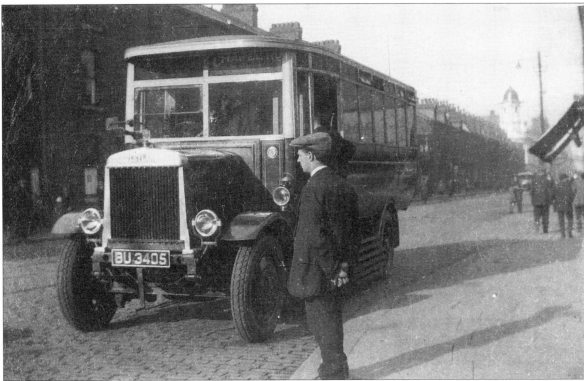

LEFT: Union Street in the late 1920's with Leyland C9 saloon No 4 (BU 3405) en-route from Greenacres to Chapel Road, to be known to generations of Oldhamers as *'th' A buz'*. *(R Marshall)*

letters were normally allocated chronologically but there were to be exceptions and re-uses. In general, joint bus and former tram services were numbered, again with some exceptions.

The first five buses comprised Leyland C9 normal-control chassis (that is, with protruding bonnet) and Leyland bodywork, 22ft 7in long, fleet-numbered 1–5. Four more Leylands, Nos 5–9, were acquired in May 1925 but these were of type C7, similar to the C9 but 24ft 10in long and seating 28. They had forward entrances, although subsequent new single deckers to 1928 had rear entrances. As with the AECs to be mentioned and two used buses acquired

in 1929, the engines of these Leylands had four cylinders although all future buses in the fleet were to have six-cylinder units. The tyres of 1-9 were pneumatic and a conventional four-speed sliding mesh or "crash" gearbox was fitted. This type of layshaft 'box, and later constant mesh and synchromesh varieties, were to be standard for Oldham until 1964, except for two batches of chassis. Leylands 1-9 were 7ft 4½in wide although by the late 1920s the normal width for a bus had become 7ft 6in and this was to remain standard until post-World War 2. These sturdy Leylands remained in service until various dates between 1930 and 1934. Appendix 3 gives fuller details of the fleet.

RIGHT: The 1925 Leyland delivery comprised four C7 models (6-9), slightly longer than the C9 type and seating 28. The destination is displayed centrally at the front and not in the nearside top light position as with the previous saloons. Dressed in typically military-style uniform with 'bandsman' collar, the driver of No 9 (BU 3675) poses proudly but presumably will leave his fingermarks on the nearside wing. *(Ribble Enthusiasts' Club)*

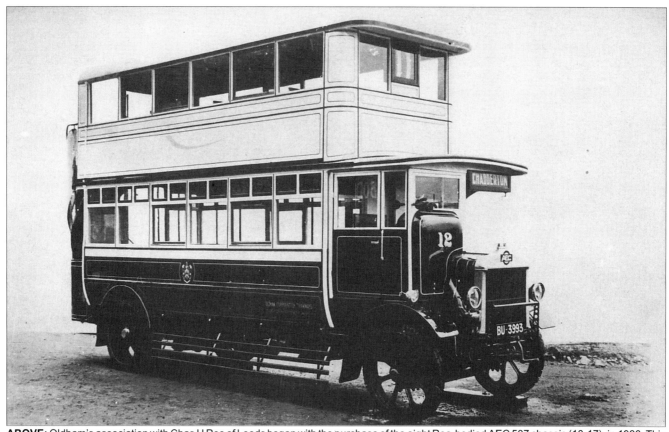

ABOVE: Oldham's association with Chas H Roe of Leeds began with the purchase of the eight Roe-bodied AEC 507 chassis (10-17), in 1926. This view of 12 clearly illustrates the tramcar-derived features of the body, together with the somewhat high dash panel and resulting shallow windscreen. The destination and service number displays are random and should not be regarded as authentic. (*The late R. Taylor collection*)

Mr Chamberlain left in April 1925 to take charge of the Leeds tramways and transport undertaking and on 28 May Mr Clement Jackson of Keighley accepted the Oldham post. On 1 August 1925, service C was commenced between Clegg Street Station and Middleton Junction. The Corporation acquired the Belgrave Mills open-top Leyland double decker at this time, numbering it 10, and from 20 August 1925 took over its Rhodes Bank - Wash Brook service, giving it the letter D. Service E, Oldham (Town Hall) - Mossley (Brookbottom),

was commenced on 23 January 1926 in conjunction with the Stalybridge, Hyde, Mossley and Dukinfield (SHMD) Joint Board. The ex-Belgrave bus was traded in against the addition of an eighth bus to an order for seven forward-control double deckers (that is, with driving position alongside the engine) of the Associated Equipment Company (AEC) 507-type, known briefly as the "Ramillies" model, Nos10-17, delivered early in 1926. Their solid-tyred spoked wheels were to be replaced by pneumatic-tyred dished ones in 1928. The 52-seat bodywork,

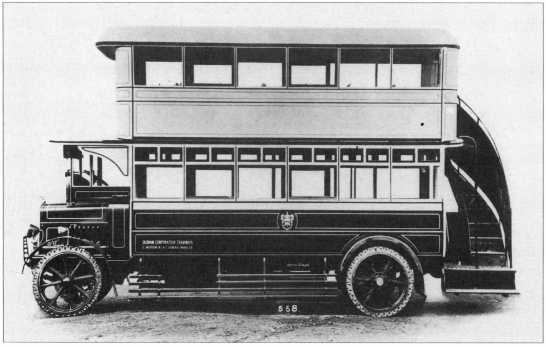

LEFT: This nearside view of 12 at Roe's premises shows the exposed platform and staircase. On the side rocker panel (ie, the lower one) the legal lettering reads Oldham Corporation Tramways - C Jackson MIAE, General Manager and, on the underframe, Speed 12mph. The solid tyres were later replaced by pneumatics. (*R. Marshall*)

top-covered but with open platform and staircase, was built by Chas H Roe of Leeds. These buses were ordered only after the Tramways Committee had visited Sheffield and Nottingham to inspect the top-covered double deck buses, one Brush-bodied AEC and three Short-bodied Dennises respectively, in those cities. Although there was confidence in trams with top covers, which leaned *into* curves, there was some apprehension about the stability of top-covered buses which leaned *out* of them. Frequently throughout its history, Oldham Corporation was to place bodywork orders with Roe. Nos10-17 were

disposed of together to the Canvey & District Motor Transport Co, Essex, in 1933.

Oldham had a brief trolleybus interlude during the mid-1920s. Southerly neighbour Ashton-under-Lyne was faced with the expense of tram track renewal on the Hathershaw - Ashton town centre section which was Ashton's part of the jointly-operated No14 Oldham (Star Inn) - Ashton tram service. Ashton decided to run "trackless trolley vehicles" and asked Oldham to do the same in order to keep the through running facility. A joint order was placed for ten

LEFT: Oldham Corporation trolleybus 2, one of a pair of Short Bros-bodied Railless chassis and part of a joint order for ten placed by Ashton-under-Lyne and Oldham Corporations. *(R. Marshall/J. J. Holmes)*

LOWER LEFT: The unusual perimeter seating arrangement of the trolleybuses is shown here in an illustration taken from a 1925 brochure issued by Railless and described as their 'Low Floor Car'. *(R Marshall/J J Holmes)*

trolleybuses with chassis built by Railless and bodywork with 36 perimeter seats by Short Bros, the parent of Railless. It was specified that they should be able to climb a 1 in 12 gradient and they were powered by two 35hp English Electric motors. Two of the vehicles were taken by Oldham and Ashton took the other eight.

The joint Oldham (Chaucer Street, near Star Inn) - Ashton (Market) service started on 26 August 1925 with a frequency of 7½ to 10 minutes. Trams on the through Hathershaw - Summit service still ran on the Hathershaw - Star Inn section, of course, and as the tram wire was also the positive wire for the trolleybuses, overtaking between trams and trolleybuses was not possible. This led to some problems and so, on 2 April 1926, motor buses replaced trams on Hathershaw–Summit although some trams still ran at peak times. Financial results from the trolleybuses were encouraging but there were many complaints from Ashton Road residents about the excessive vibration caused by the solid-tyred electric buses. Oldham was willing to allow Ashton to run the whole service if vehicles with pneumatic tyres could have been used. Suitable tyres were not available, however, and so on 5 September 1926 the "trackless trams", as they were often called, were replaced by motor buses between Hathershaw and Oldham. No 2 was subsequently dismantled and its chassis and spares sold to Ashton in 1930, the body being disposed of separately. Details of the disposal of No1 are inconclusive but it is believed to have remained at Copsterhill Road yard for some years in ever-deteriorating condition before being scrapped. Ashton continued to run trolleybuses on their section south of Hathershaw until 1938.

A new and more spacious bus garage was opened on 10 October 1926 at the north end of Henshaw Street, some 750ft above sea level and on the top of the Oldham Edge escarpment. It had to be extended just three years later to accommodate the growing fleet. Among the first new buses

to be housed at Henshaw Street were a trio of three-axle (six-wheel) normal-control double deckers with Roe 54-seat bodies and Guy BX-type chassis, delivered in November 1926 as Nos18-20. They also had open staircase and platform and although larger, due to the space taken up the protruding lengthy bonnet and by the driving cab within the lower saloon they could seat only two more than the AECs. At that time tyre technology had not advanced to the point where buses could be fitted with twin wheels on the rear axles in order to permit increased weight-carrying. An obvious answer was to fit a second rear axle and other six-wheelers were to join the Oldham fleet during the next two years. It is interesting to note that some three decades after the delivery of these first Guy six-wheelers to Oldham, the Leyland Atlantean came on to the market and within just 3ft 5in additional length it could accommodate up to 24 more passengers!

The Guy BX had been introduced in 1926 as a four-cylinder model but Oldham's 18-20 had *six*-cylinder engines (97mm bore, 130mm stroke). This was the type of engine fitted to the seven Guy normal-control, six-wheel saloons delivered at about the same time, Nos21-27, with Guy's own 32-seat bodywork. Due to the low-built chassis frame their overall height was only 8ft 7in. They were of chassis type BKX, Guy using the letter 'K' here to signify the fitting of an engine manufactured and supplied by Daimler, incorporating the Knight sleeve-valve system of American origin. 23-27 had Zenith carburettors while 21/22, and double deckers 18-20, had Daimler Multi Jet carburettors. Although Oldham records refer to 18-20 as BX models with BX chassis numbers, and not the BKX type, there is reference to them as *Guy Daimlers* which clearly confirms their engine type. The seating capacity of these Guys was low in relation to their length and was to be matched or exceeded by the slightly shorter 1930s buses which did not have the complication of a third axle.

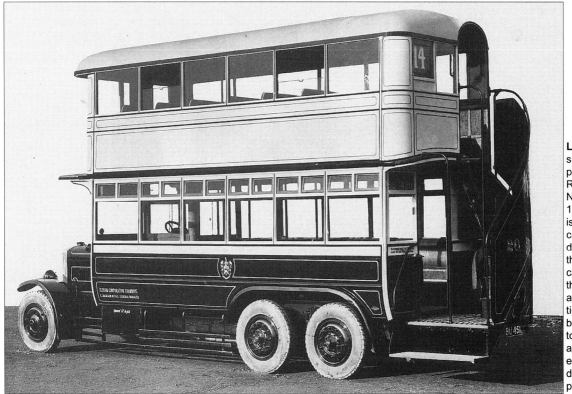

LEFT: Oldham's first six-wheelers comprised three 54-seat Roe-bodied Guy BXs, Nos18–20, built in 1926, of which No 20 is shown. The normal-control layout, with driving position behind the engine and, in this case, partitioned from the saloon, was never a popular configuration for double-deck buses. The high step to the platform and arched upper saloon entrance were typical design features of the period. *(MTMS)*

As the Oldham fleet grew, a small but significant proportion of it comprised single deckers due to the existence of low bridges on the west side of the town and in Chadderton. Although one of them, at Mills Hill on the Chadderton - Middleton boundary, was to have its headroom increased in 1934, most of the others remained unaltered into the 1990s and were too low even for lowbridge double deck buses. Of the 73 new buses entering service during 1924-32, thirty-six were single deck.

1927 saw these motor bus services inaugurated or extended between January and August:

1 Jan G Town Hall–Manor Road (new)

28 Jan D Rhodes Bank–Coalshaw Grn Rd (western end) (extension)

6 Apr A Chapel Rd–Waterhead (Heywood St) (extension)

6 Apr F Shaw–Middleton (new, entirely outside borough boundary)

30 Jul B New Hey–Woodhouses (extension; now joint with N Western)

15 Apr H Oldham–Halifax (new; joint with Halifax Corp and North Western—in competition with Ripponden & District Motor Services)

12 Aug J Oldham - Greenfield via Lees (new; joint with N Western)

On 19 July 1927 Oldham Corporation and North Western entered into an agreement setting out each one's territory and providing for joint operation, the first manifestation being the extension of service B followed soon by the commencement of service J. There were problems with service H to Halifax when larger buses were substituted for the small driver-only single deckers which could not cope with the loadings. West Riding County Council complained of damage to their roads and from 28 July 1928 Oldham buses ran between Oldham and Denshaw only. Under a zoning agreement Halifax withdrew altogether and the service continued with the North Western and Yorkshire Woollen District companies jointly, extended at both ends to become Manchester - Bradford.

In 1927, Henry Mattinson, General Manager of Manchester Corporation Tramways, proposed a system of limited-stop bus services, often described as "express", throughout the area. He wanted to encourage bus travel by making it quicker where appropriate especially over the longer

RIGHT: Guy BKX saloon 25 here carries a route board for the F service (Middleton - Streetbridge - Royton - Shaw). Presumably the second conductor is a trainee. *(Ribble Enthusiasts' Club)*

ABOVE: Chas H Roe's first saloon bodies for Oldham were those fitted to 30–32 of 1927, originally with 39 seats but later reduced to 37. Guy supplied the FCX-type chassis and No30 (BU 4840), the first of the three is pictured here. *(Ribble Enthusiasts' Club)*

distances. Many of the proposed routes were to run across Manchester city centre. Buses would stop only at tramway fare stages (where routes overlapped) and fares would be about double tram fares, with a 2d minimum. All participating operators, including Oldham, met in August 1927 and agreed to the scheme, North Western joining in 1928. The first of these services affecting Oldham began in October 1927 as Hollinwood - Urmston, altered to Hollinwood - Gatley in January 1928, operated by Manchester. A jointly-operated Ashton - Oldham - Rochdale express service was commenced between those three towns as No9 on 22 February 1928. Further detail revisions of the express services from the Oldham area to Manchester and beyond took place on 1929/30 as outlined in Appendix 1.

Below is a brief summary of the new buses, all with three axles, delivered during 1927/28. They were of forward control-layout which was to be standard until 1964.

1927		
28/29	Karrier WL6/1	Short Bros 39-seat single deck
30-32	Guy FCX	Roe 39-seat single deck
33/34	Guy FCX	Roe 56-seat double deck
1928		
35	Karrier DD6/1	Hall, Lewis 70-seat double deck
36	Guy FCX	Short Bros 72-seat double deck
37-42	Karrier CL6	Hall, Lewis 33-seat single deck
43-48	Karrier DD6	English Electric 66-seat double deck
49-56	Guy FCX	English Electric 66-seat double deck

Karrier chassis, which had air brakes acting only on the rear four wheels, were manufactured only about 18 miles away in Huddersfield although Oldham's first pair, 28/29, were sent to Rochester in Kent for fitting with Short Bros bodywork. These and Guys 30-32 had more seats than any single deckers delivered to Oldham until 1964, although the Guys had two seats removed in 1932 in compliance with

the Construction and Use Regulations introduced with the Road Traffic Act, 1930. Guy 36 had the highest seating capacity of any double decker in the fleet until 1964. 70-seat Karrier 35 was delivered late due to its being exhibited at the 1927 Commercial Motor Show in London, the first of several Oldham buses to be posed in this way over the years. Its body builders, Hall, Lewis & Co of north-west London (to become Park Royal Coachworks in 1930), used a photograph of it in their publicity material, describing it as a 72-seater. 35's engine incorporated Ricardo sleeve valves as did those of Karriers 43-48 although these engines had a smaller swept volume. English Electric of Preston, highly-regarded in the tramway field, built the bodies on 43-56. The six wheelers generally and the sleeve-valve examples in particular had an extravagant thirst for petrol and engine oil. They would frequently need topping-up with fuel or lubricant, or both, during a day's service and this was done by garage staff on the road at or near the Market Place. Eventually the police put a stop to it and other arrangements had to be made.

The Karriers were notoriously unreliable which of course added to their running costs greatly. They were the shortest-lived of any new buses added to the fleet after 1924. The six-wheelers had four-wheel drive via two differentials and it does appear that Oldham Corporation disconnected the drive from the rearmost axle. This was done in order to minimise wear and breakages of some transmission components caused by the absence of a third differential. The modification introduced a further problem, however: on a greasy or uneven surface there was some loss of adhesion, sometimes causing the driven wheels to slip during acceleration. Despite their drawbacks, the buses of those days were easily capable of exceeding the speed limit by a wide margin—even when it was raised from 12mph to 20mph in 1928. New and improved two-axle models were soon to make three-axle models obsolescent among most provincial operators.

LEFT: The final new Oldham buses with open rear platform and staircase were Guy FCX models 33/34, acquired in 1927. Present-day automatic bus-washing equipment would leave parts of the Roe 56-seat body untouched but this scene shows 33 having a thorough job done on it in Henshaw Street garage. *(GMTS)*

It should not be inferred, incidentally, that 1920's buses were poor in general: Oldham just had some particularly unreliable types.

The need for so many new buses was due in part to the withdrawal of some tram services where costly track renewal was becoming necessary. Lees saw its last tram on 1 May 1928, buses taking over on a new service O, Market Place - Grotton, next day. Buses then replaced trams between Market Place and Grains Bar from 24 December 1928. Bus service 5 went all the way, 6 terminated at Moorside, and both were to be co-ordinated with the H to Denshaw on 27 August 1930.

BELOW: The largest Guy, 36, and rival of Karrier 35, is seen from just inside Henshaw Street garage. New in 1928 and of type FCX with 72-seat Short Bros body, it shows a discordant relationship between the offside of the cab and the front of the lower saloon. The bus behind and to the right is one of the 1927 pair of Guy FCX double deckers and the saloon just visible beyond that is one of the four Leyland C7s of 1925. *(Ribble Enthusiasts' Club)*

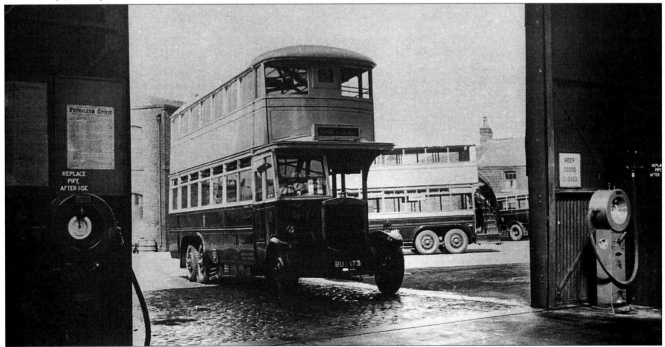

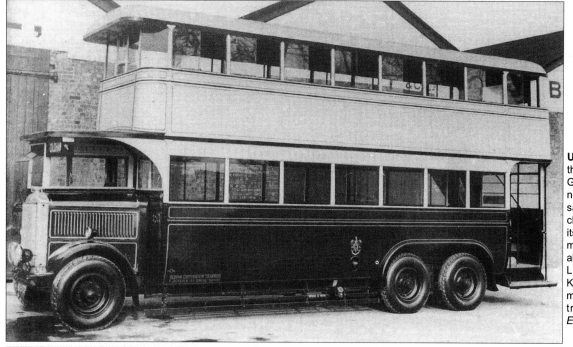

UPPER LEFT: Although the offside cab area of Guy 36 was messy, this nearside view of the same bus shows most clearly how the lines of its Short Bros body were more up-to-date generally than those of the Hall, Lewis body fitted to Karrier 35 which owed more to tramcar design tradition. *(Ribble Enthusiasts' Club)*

CENTRE LEFT: Karrier chassis were Huddersfield-built and the largest example delivered to Oldham was the sole DD6/1 in the fleet, 35, which was exhibited on the stand of its bodybuilders, Hall, Lewis & Co of London, at the 1927 Commercial Motor Show at Olympia. The Hall, Lewis sedan chair and scroll motif, subsequently adopted by their successor, Park Royal Coachworks, appears above the name Oldham in the legal lettering on the lower saloon panelling of the 70-seat bodywork. *(Ribble Enthusiasts' Club)*

LOWER LEFT: Oldham's six Karrier CL6 saloons of 1928 (37-42) had Hall, Lewis 33-seat bodywork of much more futuristic styling than that of Karrier double decker 35. The two-aperture destination and route display as shown by 39 is noteworthy. Was the design of the rear wings inspired by the splashers over the coupled wheels of H Wainwright's class D steam locomotives on the former South Eastern & Chatham Railway? *(R. Marshall)*

When Mr Clement Jackson resigned on 28 November 1928 to become General Manager at Plymouth he was succeeded immediately by Mr J F Richards, Oldham's Rolling Stock Superintendent. Just over a year later, on 9 December 1929, the Corporation received two used single deck buses which were part of the distribution from a successful operator of long-distance coach services and Manchester-area bus routes, J R Tognarelli of Bolton. This concern was acquired for £24,000 by the Corporations of Manchester, Salford, Bolton and Oldham and the Lancashire United Transport & Power Co Ltd. One of Tognarelli's services ran between Manchester (Mayes Street) and Chadderton (Burnley Lane/Garforth Street) and this

continued in place of the Royton (Summit) - Manchester (Lower Mosley Street) service from 9 December 1929 for six months. Then on 19 May 1930 it was merged with the No2 New Hey service to run New Hey - Manchester (Lower Mosley Street) via Shaw, Royton and Chadderton as service 2. The two acquired buses, numbered 57/58 in the Oldham fleet, had Associated Daimler Co (ADC) type 426 chassis and were believed new in December 1928 and February 1929, with bodywork by Bell of Doncaster and Burlingham of Blackpool respectively (although one source states Bell for both). ADC was a short-lived venture which had been set up in 1926 to market AEC and Daimler products, AEC building the 426 model. Oldham's pair were withdrawn in 1934.

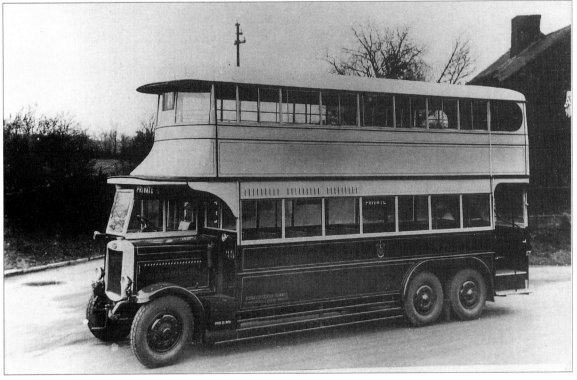

Oldham Corporation Tramways. FARE LIST

CHAPEL ROAD & GREENACRES

Chapel Road (0)

- Grange Avenue (1)

1d. - Windsor Road (2)

1½d. 1d. - Lee Street (3)

2d. 1½d. 1d. - Star Inn (4)

2½d. 2d. 1½d. 1d. - Rhodes Bank (5)

3d. 2½d. 2d. 1½d. 1d. - Cross Street (6)

3½d. 3d. 2½d. 2d. 1½d. 1d. - Dunkerley Street (7)

4d. 3½d. 3d. 2½d. 2d. 1½d. 1d. - Greenacres Cemetery (8)

CHILDREN'S FARES :- One Child (under 5 years) not occupying a seat FREE. Any additional Child (under 14 years) HALF-FARE.

Children, between 5 and 14 years of age HALF-FARE.

SCHOLARS' FARES :- Scholars under 16 years of age, going to or from school up to 9-0 a.m., between noon and 2-0 p.m., and between 4-0 and 5-30 p.m., are charged Children's Fares. A charge of 1d. is made for the carriage of each Dog.

PASSENGERS' LUGGAGE :- Personal Luggage, up to 28 lbs. :- FREE. Packages exceeding 28 lbs., or Packages of a bulky nature, 2d each.

Wallshaw Depot,
OLDHAM,
March 25th, 1931.

J. F. RICHARDS,
General Manager & Engineer.

Mr Richards was called upon to defend his Department's record when on 7 May 1930 Alderman Frith, not a member of the Tramways Committee, made allegations at a Council meeting about bus maintenance. These were reported in the Oldham Evening Chronicle and Standard (as it then was) and on 14 May Mr Richards presented a report to the Tramways Committee. He refuted charges of neglect, danger and dirt, pointing out the following:

• Only 10 days previously, 55 of the 58 buses had been passed by the Borough Hackney Carriage Inspectors, the remaining three being overhauled.

• While the mechanics were on short time, safety was not jeopardised as their total weekly hours were 1,333 which was only 30 less than normal, and approximating to 23 hours per bus, only about half an hour less than normal.

• Under a new and rigorous system, each bus had a "dock" overhaul every 11,500 miles and a complete overhaul every 38,500* miles (previous year's figure 45,000), leading to a fall in defects from 103 a month to 87.

• The bus fleet age profile was: 28% up to 2 yrs old, 26% up to 3, 17% up to 4, 14% up to 4½, 15% more than 4½.

*Author's note: this may be compared, for example, with about 50,000 miles for Birmingham Corporation and about 60,000 for the North Western Road Car Company at that time.

Regarding short-time working, Oldham had been affected adversely for some 18 months by the trade depression together with the Indian market boycott of British cotton goods. Local unemployment was high and passenger transport loadings low during 1928-32. Transport employees' wages were cut and various economy measures implemented, including the removal of self-starters from those newer buses that had them. Matters did not improve significantly until the mid-1930s.

It is enlightening to examine the faults that needed rectification on the petrol-engined 1920s buses. The records for 13 September 1930, amplified below, reveal that five were out of service. This figure represented 8.6 per cent which was not a bad situation.

Fleet No	Chassis type	Body type	Reason out of service
2	Leyland C9	sd	Engine being rebuilt following breakage of crankshaft 3 days earlier.
31	Guy FCX	sd	Brought in from service 11am. Main frame front crossmember broken.
48	Karrier DD6	dd	Defective sleeve in engine; covered by maker's guarantee. Information passed to Karrier with request for soon-as-possible repair.
52	Guy FCX	dd	Complete overhaul and repaint
57	ADC 426	sd	Breakage of timing chain tensioning device previous day

In 1930 the diesel engine era was still three years away for Oldham and it may be appropriate at this point compare the reliability of the 1920s buses with those that were to come during the decade to follow. The comparison in the table below is between the financial years 1929/30 with 58 petrol-engined buses and 1937/38 with 150 diesel-engined and only 16 petrol-engined buses.

Year	Total miles operated	Miles lost due to defects	Service miles per lost mile (avge)	Change-overs due to defects	Service miles per change-over (avge)	Repair & maint cost/bus mile
1929/30	1,776,780	7,413	240	2,252	789	4.137d (= 1.724p)
1937/38	3,889,870	216	17,967	426	9,131	1.258d (= 0.524p)

In the late 1920s, the two chassis manufacturing market leaders arrived at winning formulae, resulting in the Leyland Titan and Tiger, introduced late 1927, and the AEC Regent and Regal, introduced in 1929. These models offered standards of comfort, reliability and economy far superior to those of Oldham's buses then in service. The motor bus was maturing and new standards were being set, shortly to take a leap forward in economy with the widespread adoption of the diesel engine. Oldham emerged from the obsolescent six-wheel age and entered the new era in 1931 when the first Leyland Tiger type TS3 saloons entered service, wearing the new livery of white and crimson lake (always officially described as this and never as maroon or chocolate, although in later years suppliers' labels called it "Oldham red"). Leyland's 26ft-long TS3 model, with 16ft 6in wheelbase, had a 6.8-litre overhead-camshaft petrol engine that

was so quiet and vibration-free that passengers may have thought it had been switched off when in fact it was idling. The later TS4 model was built to the two-axle single deck legal maximum length of 27ft 6in, its wheelbase was 17ft 6in long and it had the more powerful 7.6-litre version of the engine. Both types had ample power for Oldham's gradients and were easily capable of exceeding the overall bus and coach speed limit, raised by 10mph to 30mph in 1931.

Oldham's petrol-engined Tigers, with their body types, were as summarised here:

1931	59-62	TS3	Roe — 31-seat
1932	63-66	TS4	Roe — 33-seat
	67	TS4	Shearing & Crabtree—31-seat

Chas H Roe was developing an excellent reputation for high-quality, well-finished teak-framed products that were to prove durable. The Leeds concern was to become Oldham's principal supplier of bodywork over the next 38 years, building 146 bodies (68 per cent) on the 214 chassis ordered pre-war. Shearing and Crabtree, builders of the body on Tiger 67, were a local concern based in Moorhey Street, Oldham, producing motor vehicle bodies during 1931-37. One partner,

UPPER LEFT: Leyland's Tiger TS3-type had a wheelbase of 16ft 6in to accept 26ft-long bodywork. Third of Oldham's four examples, 61 poses at Roe's Cross Gates Carriage Works in Leeds before delivery in 1931. The famous Roe scroll transfer is visible on the waistrail behind the entrance. Crimson lake has now replaced the dark blue livery and the General Manager is John Frederick Richards. A 31-seater, the bus carries a route board for the New Hey - Manchester limited-stop service. (The late R. Taylor collection)

LEFT: This wonderfully atmospheric shot of Oldham Market Place shows 62, a Leyland Tiger TS3, on limited-stop service 13 (Manchester - Uppermill via Scouthead) in the 1930s. On the left, car 111 is about to commence a journey on tram route 11 to Hollinwood via Werneth. (R. Marshall)

Herbert Shearing, also operated coaches from a garage in Lees Road nearby, later moving from Oldham. By the 1990s, his enterprise was to grow into Europe's largest holiday coach tour operator. Another kind of sizeable organisation in the form of a single transport board for the Manchester area many have been created, had there been a positive result from an Oldham Tramways Committee agenda item in 1931. Nothing of the kind was to exist until the SELNEC PTA and PTE were formed in 1969 and the subject is covered after the end of the Oldham undertaking's chronological story.

The Leyland Tiger's double deck counterpart was the Titan, powered by the same engine. Successive models of Titan were to form the backbone of the Oldham fleet throughout the rest of its existence. Eight TD2 models (68-75) were acquired in 1932, fitted with Leyland's own "Hybridge" 51-seat bodywork sporting the then characteristic upper saloon "piano-front".

Fuel economy always exercised the minds of transport managers and from the late 1920s a few enterprising opera-

tors experimented with "compression-ignition" ("CI") or "oil" engines that used heavy oil as fuel, giving much greater economy. The term "diesel" was not widely used at that time when First World War memories were still fresh, because of its German connotations. In 1930, Oldham Tramways Committee had gone to Sheffield by invitation to inspect two of the city's buses that had been fitted experimentally with diesels. One was a 1929 Karrier WL6/1 six-wheel saloon powered by a Mercedes-Benz 6.46-litre unit. The other was a 1930 Crossley Condor four-wheel double decker with an 8.4-litre Gardner 6L2 light marine engine, two other similarly-treated Crossleys running in Leeds and Manchester. Oldham took a cautious approach,

doing nothing until 1932 when Leyland and Crossley diesel demonstrators were tried, each with the chassis-maker's own diesel engine. Crossley Motors, then of Gorton, Manchester, had produced a 9.12-litre diesel engine in December 1930. Leyland's overhead-camshaft, pot-cavity 8.1-litre unit had first been revealed in 1931, the external dimensions being the same as those of the equivalent petrol engine in the interests of interchangeability. Early in 1933, Oldham converted a Guy to run on creosote oil and although given trials it did not operate in service and was returned to original form. A decision was also made to fit a Leyland diesel experimentally to Titan 72, only nine months old, and this bus did re-enter service, on 27 January

BELOW: Oldham's first buses delivered with diesel engines were 1932 order of eight Titan TD2 models (10-17—re-used numbers) with 54-seat English Electric bodywork. In this garage line-up, of the eleven buses in the front row, the first, third, fifth, sixth, eighth and ninth are TD2s of the 10-17 batch and the remainder are later Roe-bodied TD3s. The bus nearest the camera is TD2 No16, standing in front of TD3 No94, affording an opportunity to identify the differences in appearance of frontally-similar English Electric and Roe bodywork. Note the number of side windows, the treatment of the cab offside, the rake of the upper saloon front windows and the roof contours. (Ribble Enthusiasts' Club)

1933. It was an undoubted success. Over the next five months, 72 covered up to 1,000 miles a week and averaged 9.48 miles per gallon. The average petrol consumption for the rest of the fleet was only 5.2mpg. Moreover, petrol was then costing the Corporation approximately 1s 5d a gallon (about 7p), including 4d tax, compared with untaxed diesel fuel oil at only around 5d (just over 2p). Although the diesel engine was more expensive to buy, even when the fuel was taxed in 1935 its overall economy remained much superior.

Oldham standardised on diesel engines from 1933 with the delivery of eight more Titan TD2s (10-17) and nine Roe-bodied 32-seat Tiger TS4s (21-29) in July and August. The TD2s had 54-seat bodywork built by English Electric which was to become Oldham's secondary bus body supplier for several years. These bodies introduced that unusual Oldham characteristic, the offside destination indicator, positioned at first in a lower saloon window but subsequently in the rearmost upper saloon panel above the staircase.

tramway revenue had been £227,000 compared with £12,000 from the buses. By 1930 those figures had become £192,000 and £105,000 respectively, falling by about ten and five per cent in 1931 due to the slump. The growing role of the bus led to a change of name of the Tramways Committee to the Passenger Transport Committee from 6 July 1933. Although tram services to Lees and Grains Bar had been abandoned in 1928, the Committee did not adopt a policy of general tramway abolition until 1934. It was intended to complete the programme during 1935-39 but of course the war intervened. As mentioned earlier, Appendix 1 lists the relevant details.

In order to decide on bus purchasing policy in anticipation of the tramway replacement programme, a Crossley Mancunian and a Leyland Titan TD3 (57/58) were acquired for comparison in 1934. The Crossley had its builder's own 9.12-litre VR6-type engine and a Roe 53-seat body. The Leyland diesel as fitted to 58 had been increased

ABOVE: Leyland Titan TD2, No 16, is seen again during World War 2 when on hire to Chepstow-based Red & White Motor Services, in company with one of their Albion saloons. The Oldham bus is somewhat bedraggled, with paint flaking from the roof and dirty white blackout markings on the front wings and dumb irons. Headlamp masks and 'pinhole' sidelight apertures are noteworthy. *(R. Marshall)*

During that period there a generally similar "recessed V-front" upper saloon profile characterised Roe, English Electric, Short Bros and Burlingham double deck bodies, the first two named being in Oldham's fleet and giving it a somewhat standardised appearance. There were, however, detail differences including five-bay construction used by Roe along with a more deeply-arched roof and the highly characteristic "proud" waistrails to both saloons, compared with six-bay English Electric bodies which had a slight "bustle" effect to rear profile.

Although the growth of Oldham's bus network from 1924 had been fairly rapid, the trams had continued to carry most of the load along the main arteries. In 1926 the

in swept volume to 8.6 litres, the chassis featured the new and neater Leyland radiator shell and it bore an English Electric 54-seat body (the seating difference being explained by the need to keep the Crossley, which had a higher unladen weight, within the prevailing 10-ton gross weight limit). While the Crossley engine was marginally superior in nominal power output it earned a poor reputation for reliability and economy among diesels. The Leyland unit was renowned for smooth running at higher speeds, its subdued sound blending harmoniously with the aural effects of the constant-mesh gearbox which incorporated the so-called "silent third" speed. These humming and crooning accompaniments to travel characterised all Leyland Titans and Tigers

ABOVE: Oldham's first and experimental Crossley was this 1934 Mancunian model, No 57 (BU 7945), built at Gorton, Manchester, with Roe bodywork seating 53 when new. Unlike other buses in the fleet, its fuel filler was on the nearside. The angle of the steering wheel is noteworthy as is the use of *Passenger Transport* in place of Tramways in the legal lettering on the foremost nearside lower saloon panel. It was withdrawn in 1949 and so outlasted its rival, Leyland Titan TD3 No58, by one year. *(The late R. Taylor collection)*

with this combination of units until pre-war designs were superseded. Oldham's chassis preference became clear. The Corporation was to order a further 164 Leyland double deckers but only five Crossleys until the outbreak of war.

A further three Tigers entered service (18-20) in 1934. These were of the TS6 type (equivalent to the Titan TD3) and had Roe 32-seat fully-fronted bodywork (that is, the panelling enveloped the bonnet and front nearside wing

RIGHT: Challenger to Crossley Mancunian 57 was 58 (BU7946), a Leyland Titan TD3, also new in 1934, with an English Electric 54-seat body. The sunshine of high summer beams as 58 climbs Yorkshire Street, viewed from the Town Hall steps and barely a minute away from its Market Place destination. In hot pursuit is 1933 Tiger TS4 No23 with Roe 32-seat bodywork. All visible windows of both buses are fully open, as is the sun roof of the contemporary Morris Ten saloon car. Note the tidier appearance of the Titan's bonnet, radiator and wings compared with earlier types illustrated. *(Ribble Enthusiasts' Club)*

ABOVE: The trio of 1934 Leyland TS6 Tigers (18-20) had full-fronted Roe bodywork, exemplified here by 20 (BU 8256). This one was intended for permanent use on limited-stop service 10 (Manchester - Greenfield) as shown on the red route glasses. *(The late R. Taylor collection)*

area, there being no cut-away section). They were fitted with Clayton heaters and saloon heating became part of Oldham's standard specification in later years. Intended for Manchester express work, they carried route information on red-tinted glasses above three of the windows on each side. Of course these could not be changed and so the buses were confined as follows: 18 to Uppermill (services 13/14), 19 to New Hey (2) and 20 Greenfield (10). During the war, the route glasses were overpainted which allowed flexibility of allocation.

Six Roe-bodied TD3 Titans (30-35) were placed in service at about the same time as the TS6s. Nos33/35 had 53 seats while the rest had 54. Again, this was due to differences in their individual unladen weights. The five further Crossleys already mentioned were delivered in December 1934 (Nos1-5) and stored until June 1935 when the first phase of tramway replacement was implemented. Roe-bodied, the Crossleys were part of the large 1934/35 intake, No4 with 52 seats and the others with 53. While the Crossley Mancunian of that era may have had an imposing radiator shell, other features were becoming anachronistic. The centrally-positioned accelerator pedal and well raked-

BELOW: Oldham's largest delivery of buses before 1939 comprised the 26 Leyland TD3 Titans with Roe 54-seat bodywork (76-101) placed in service during 1935, assembled here numerically. Just inside the Henshaw Street garage entrance are the five Crossleys (1-5). Note the hinged vents in the upper saloon front windows of the Leylands. *(GMTS)*

back steering column were more in keeping with 1920s practice, for instance (although steering column fashion was to change back again years later). With such a minority in a mixed fleet, driving was an interesting if at times confusing experience. The Crossley engines worked on the Ricardo indirect injection system and 1-5, probably also 57, were altered to direct injection soon after World War 2. It seems clear that the pre-war Crossleys were a headache to the Passenger Transport Department. They proved unpopular with drivers and would be changed over for other types frequently. By early post-war years they had accrued much lower mileage than average but their bodies were structurally sound and they were fit for considerably longer service. They soldiered on, mostly doing peak time duties until 1949 (57) and 1950 (1-5).

Soon after the arrival of Crossleys 1-5, a further 26 Roe-bodied 54-seat Leyland TD3s commenced delivery over a three-month period (76-101). While records are contradictory, circumstantial evidence suggests that 76-79 entered service on 1 January 1935. It is conclusive, however, that at least 80-101 were stored until June for the same reason as Crossleys 1-5. Some of Leylands 76-101 had brackets fitted at the front, enabling route description boards to be carried for the long and sinuous jointly-operated 59 route, Manchester (Cannon Street) - Shaw (Wren's Nest), which in part replaced two tramway sections. The use of the boards did not last long. All of 76-101 had hinged forward-facing window vents at the upper saloon front, not to be seen on future Oldham buses until the 1950s and then in a different form.

Further substantial orders were placed with Leyland for successive TD models of Titan, each type incorporating some features different from those of its predecessor but all having the same basic engine and gearbox. The shape of the dumb irons was an external identification point, those of the TD3 and TD4 being rounded, with a detail difference, and those of the TD5 flat-fronted. Roe and English Electric bodies were of composite construction (that is, timber and

RIGHT: Another coachbuilder specialising in metal-framed bodywork was the Metropolitan-Cammell Carriage & Wagon Co of Birmingham, which built just one body for Oldham in pre-war years. This was on a Leyland Titan TD4 chassis, 105, entering service in 1936. Here it illustrates the outline that was to be a Metro-Cammell characteristic, with perhaps some later refinement, until the 1950s. Numerically it was Oldham's first 56-seater, although not the first to go into service, and this figure was to be the fleet's double deck standard until 1957. (R. Marshall)

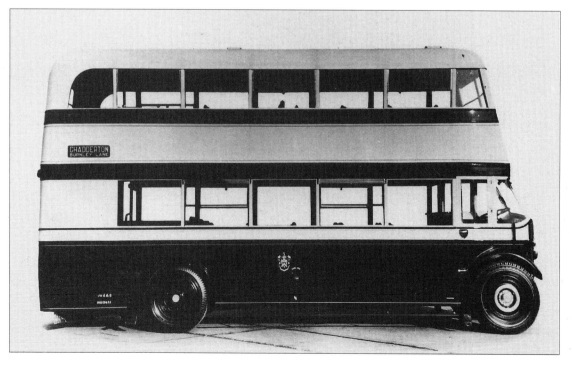

ABOVE: 116, a further 1936 Leyland TD4, had experimental metal-framed bodywork by Roe which could be distinguished from teak-framed products by the radiused lower corners to the windows, radiused destination apertures and the absence of the characteristic ventilator covers with flared ends above the lower saloon side windows. The unladen weight was about the same as that for most other Oldham buses new at that time, approximately 6˚ tons. *(R. Marshall)*

metal) except for the Roe body of 116, which was metal-framed. It could be distinguished by the radiused lower corners of the windows. Four other metal-framed bodies were acquired, three V-fronted six-bay ones by Leyland and one five-bay example built by Metropolitan-Cammell Carriage & Wagon of Birmingham. No further MCCW products were to be obtained until 1955 but six more Leyland bodies were bought in 1938, the V-front style having been abandoned two years previously in favour of a well-proportioned five-bay design with elegantly-curving front profile. Most Leyland and Roe bodies of this period gave excellent value for money, the Leylands lasting for nearly 20 years and some of the Roes even longer.

In 1936, Roe also modernised its design, dropping the "recessed V-front" in favour of a smoothly curving and virtually unbroken profile, first seen in Oldham on 126-131. Then from 1937 Roe included its patent "safety staircase" which, although of the usual eight steps, incorporated two landings where the ascending passenger made 90-degree left turns, the lower one one the second step and the upper one on the seventh. This layout may be described as "2-5-1". The bottom step was about two feet further away than previously from the platform edge, almost eliminating the risk of a fall down the stairs and out of the bus. A distinctively-shaped staircase window on the offside quickly identified buses fitted with this feature. As the staircase encroached slightly into the lower saloon, the usual inward-facing bench seat over the offside rear wheelarch accommodated two instead of three. The lost seat was regained by making the rearmost upper saloon seat triple instead of double. English Electric did not update its

composite body design at this time and it looked old-fashioned alongside the 1936-onwards Roe and Leyland outlines.

The remaining 1935-41 Leyland deliveries were complex and are summarised in this tabulation:

1935	102-104	TD4	Leyland
	106-109	TD4	English Electric*
	110-115	TD4	Roe
	117-119	TD4	Roe
1936	105	TD4	Metro-Cammell
	36-41	TD4	English Electric
	42-47, 116	TD4	Roe
	120-125	TD4	English Electric
	126-131	TD4	Roe+
1937	132-152	TD5	English Electric
	153-167	TD5	Roe♦
1938	174-179	TD5	Leyland
1939-41	180-226	TD5	Roe

*First new 56-seaters
+First with curving front profile
♦First with "safety staircase"

Although 102-104 had only 52 seats, with the raising of the gross weight limit for two-axle buses from 10 to 10$\frac{1}{2}$ tons it was possible for those delivered from late 1935 to have 56 seats which was to be standard although not universal for Oldham's double deckers until 1954. The usual distribution was 30 in the upper saloon and 26 below but on Roe "safety staircase" bodies it was 31/25. Many earlier buses were fitted with more seats as detailed in Appendix 3.

Leylands 106-119, delivered August - December 1935 (except for 116) were needed in readiness for the replacement of trams on the Market Place - Hollins - Hollinwood section on 22 December. However, there also had been an

ABOVE: The nineteen English Electric-bodied Leyland Titan TD4s of 1935/36 included 117, shown leaving Wallshaw Street garage and displaying 'HERON STREET, HOLLINS' which meant that it was not terminating at Heron Street's junctions with Chamber Road or Manchester Road. *(R. Marshall)*

RIGHT: This photograph of No 40 was intended to illustrate the dent to the offside wing but it captures the detail of the cab frontal area of the English Electric body as fitted to a Leyland TD4. The tasteful style of the fleet numeral is also shown to good effect. *(Courtesy J. J. Holmes)*

BELOW: English Electric bodywork of he 1930s had a noticeable rake to the rear profile, starting from below platform window-level with a slight indentation at the contour of the dark band above. 122, a 1936 TD4, illustrates this clearly. Noteworthy also are the two tail lamps, a stop light, rear direction indicator, two registration numbers and unclosed V-shape of the upper saloon rain guttering. *(Ribble Enthusiasts' Club)*

upsurge in bus passenger traffic which increased the need for new vehicles. Six further Leylands (three each bodied by Roe and English Electric) were therefore added to existing orders for inclusion among the 1936 deliveries and, as an immediate palliative, two Crossleys and a Leyland hired from their makers. Another network development was the commencement on 10 April 1936 of an Oldham - Stalybridge service, which Oldham designated N, routed via Pitses and Hurst on the east side of Ashton. Joint partners were Ashton Corporation and the Stalybridge, Hyde, Mossley and Dukinfield Joint Board. The solitary bus required was supplied in turn by agreement between the partners. Then on 7 November 1937, buses replaced trams on the Circular service (Town Hall - Glodwick Road - Park Road - Town Hall) and on the Hathershaw - Summit route. Further changes to the latter took place on 19 February 1939 and are summarised in Appendix 1.

Late in 1936 there was concern again about a possible shortage of buses due to increased loadings. The Corporation ordered twelve English Electric-bodied Leylands with-

out inviting competitive tenders for the bodies which, although contrary to Council standing orders, was considered justified by the urgency. Then on 24 March 1937 an application was made to the Ministry of Transport (MoT) for a loan sanction in respect of a further 30 new buses. The Chairman and General Manager were summoned to the Ministry to explain why previously the Corporation had not invited tenders for the twelve bodies mentioned. Not satisfied, the MoT approved the full amount of £27,217 for 30 chassis but only £22,440 for 30 bodies which left a shortfall of nearly £3,000 to be met out of revenue. Oldham Passenger Transport Committee protested and referred the ruling to the Municipal Passenger Transport Association, all to no avail. The buses concerned in these matters were the twelve English Electric-bodied Leylands plus a further nine (132-152), 15 Roe Leylands (153-167) and the six other buses not mentioned in the 1935-41 tabulation.

These half-dozen vehicles were 1937 Roe-bodied Daimler COG6 chassis (168-173). They were powered by the Gardner 6LW 8.4-litre engine, manufactured at Patricroft,

UPPER: By the time the Leyland Titan TD5 succeeded the TD4 in 1937, the principal builders of double deck bodywork had abandoned the 'recessed V-front' style and six-bay construction. English Electric was an exception although soon to produce its own five-bay design with curving front profile, Oldham not taking any examples. Nos 132–152, of which 147 is depicted here in an elevated position, were rare examples of the new marque of chassis fitted with the obsolescent style of body. *(R. Marshall)*

CENTRE: The Roe patent 'safety staircase', introduced at the end of 1936, was a feature of all that builder's double deck bodies for Oldham from the 1937 delivery to the end of the rear-entrance era in the late 1950s, although some such buses remained in service until the mid-1970s. In this picture, 167, a 1937 Leyland Titan TD5, illustrates how the first landing was on the second stair, enabling the bottom stair to be further from the platform, so enhancing safety and creating more circulation space. There were still 56 seats but these were split 31-over-25 instead of 30/26. *(GMTS)*

LOWER LEFT: 167 is seen again, now in later years and loading for Waterhead in High Street from which the names of Hardcastle, Hudson, Flack, like Leyland Titans, have disappeared. Also gone in the picture is the continuous metal louvre above the upper saloon windows of the bus. *(R. Marshall)*

LEFT: The light grey exhaust smoke from 170, a Coventry-built Daimler COG6 with Roe body, reveals that its Gardner 6LW engine is still cold as the bus comes down Wallshaw Street from the garage at the start of the afternoon peak, similar bus 172 following. It is just possible to see the preselector lever on the offside of the steering column, and the nut-guard ring on the front wheel is worthy of note. The six Daimlers (168-173) were a little heavier than their Leyland contemporaries and so they had a non-standard seating capacity of 54 in order to keep within the prevailing gross weight limit. *(J. Fozard)*

Eccles, and transmission was through a fluid flywheel (a form of hydro-dynamic coupling developed by Daimler in the late 1920s from Vulcan-Sinclair patents) and four-speed preselective epicyclic gearbox giving quick and easy changes. The preselector lever, set in a quadrant on the right of the steering column, was moved to the required position in advance. Changes were effected by depressing the gear-change pedal which looked like a conventional clutch pedal. A point of which to beware was that unless the driver depressed it the full length of its travel it would kick back beyond its normal position, with potentially painful consequences. The bus would then be in a false neutral and much effort would be needed to push the pedal back. Although an order for Daimler saloons was to be placed in 1940, they were not available during the war and the order was eventually amended. Daimlers 168-173 seated only 54 due to their slightly greater increased weight compared with the Leylands. They spent much of their time on the A service (Chapel Road - Greenacres) where their quick gear-changes were an asset eastbound on the arduous climbs of Chamber Road and the less steep but longer ascent of Greenacres Road. These buses were unusual among Daimlers in having polished front wheel nut guard rings. Despite the legendary fuel economy and reliability of the marque, no more Gardner-engined buses were to enter the Oldham fleet.

RIGHT: As mentioned previously, Leyland bodywork was a minority make in Oldham and only six of the 89 TD5s and three of the 42 TD4s had it. In the line-up seen here, the leader is all-Leyland TD5 No179, with two similar Roe-bodied chassis behind and a post-war PD1 fourth in line. Note that the off-side destination indicator is positioned differently on the Leyland body. *(R. Marshall)*

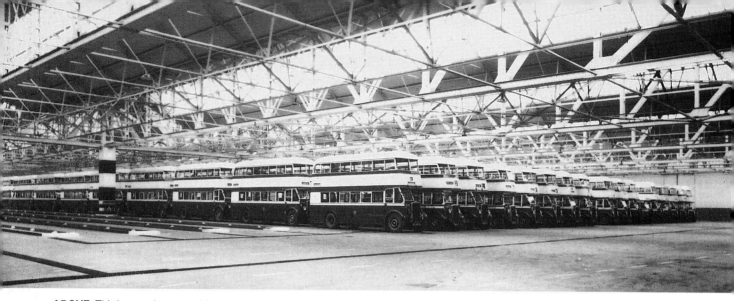

ABOVE: This impressive assembly was photographed on 26 June 1938, four weeks after the official opening of Wallshaw Street garage. All except four of the buses visible are Leyland TD4s or TD5s, that nearest the camera being English Electric-bodied TD4 No 109. Note the lane markings and the uncluttered nature of the building though the use of traditional materials has precluded the provision of a pillar-free structure. Three of the buses on the front row have brackets to receive a slip-board below the front destination aperture. *(Courtesy J. J. Holmes)*

Only six buses were delivered in 1938, Leyland TD5s again but this time with Leyland metal-framed bodywork and numbered 174–179. This builder now abandoned the V-fronted profile almost two-years previously in favour of what many commentators have regarded as a classically elegant design. The 56 seats were distributed 30-over-26 and these also gave value for money, lasting 18 to 20 years. By this time the bus fleet had outgrown its home and so on 23 May 1938 a new garage was opened at Wallshaw Street next to the tram shed. There was room for 300 buses and creditably the building also included a dining hall to seat 180, an assembly room to seat 540, sports facilities, a reading room and a bar. The wild and windy Henshaw Street site was sold and the building subsequently demolished.

The first members of the 47-strong contingent of Roe-bodied Leyland TD5s (180-226), Oldham's largest-ever order, arrived a few days after war was declared on 3 September 1939 and delivery continued until early 1941. They had moquette-covered seats throughout, signal buzzers instead of bells and, not to become standard with Roe until post-war, radiused lower corners to their side windows and elsewhere. Such a large number was intended to replace the remaining trams but initially the buses were placed in store. The need to conserve imported fuels dictated that the trams should remain

on the long and jointly-operated Waterhead–Manchester route although dispensation was obtained to withdraw the cross-suburban Hollinwood–Shaw route, which needed expensive track repairs, on 2 December 1939. Some of the new buses released older buses to go on loan to other operators as set out in Appendix 3. During the 1930s the Oldham fleet had increased from 58 to 166 buses as at 31 March 1939. The final batch of TD5s brought the total to 213, an increase of some 360 per cent since 1930.

Nos180-226 then entered service as given here:

Dec 39:	180–199
Aug 40:	220–223
Oct 40:	224/225
Nov 40:	200–209/226
Jan 41:	210–219

This large quantity of TD5s was to last until 1957-58. Within weeks of its planned withdrawal, 209 contrived to extend its life by decapitating itself under Bower Lane bridge at Hollinwood, like so many others, while out of service. The roof was chopped off neatly in one piece and not a window was broken. Old 209 was then converted into a breakdown tender wearing an all-over garb of crimson lake. It served for another ten years, affectionately nick-named "*Red Biddy*".

LEFT: Oldham's largest single order was for 47 Leyland Titan TD5 chassis with Roe bodies (180-226) which were placed in service during 1939-41. They differed from earlier Roe bodies in having individual glass louvres over the upper saloon half-drop windows rather than a full-length metal louvre. Other unusual features were the radii to the lower corners of the side windows and to all corners of the upper saloon forward-facing windows. In this scene, the conductor of 213 has come to the front for a word with his mate as they pause at Henshaw Street, outside the covered market which was later burned down. *(W. J. Haynes)*

The delivery of so many new buses early in World War 2 gave Oldham the advantage of a low fleet age profile. Increased employment on essential war-effort production caused a marked rise in tram and bus and travel, the decline in private motoring due to fuel rationing adding a little to this. Although Oldham was not to suffer the discomforts of the so-called utility buses produced from about mid-way through the war, like other operators it had to curtail services because of reduced fuel supplies and later for other reasons. The manufacture of new vehicles and equipment were controlled by the Ministry of Supply (MoS). Transport was regulated by the Ministry of War Transport (MoWT) through the Chairman of the Traffic Commissioners in each area who was redesignated Regional Transport Commissioner during the war. For the North-west Area he was Sir William Chamberlain, formerly Oldham's General Manager and an Oldham resident during the war.

> ### Summary of early changes to
> ### OLDHAM'S WARTIME SERVICES
> **24 Sep 39:** All frequencies reduced. Some services suspended 9am-noon weekdays. Works journeys not affected.
> **22 Nov 39:** Following appeal to Commissioner, some restoration of cuts. Most afternoon - early evening frequencies increased. Some duplication of busiest journeys.
> **3 Dec 39:** Buses replace trams, Hollinwood - Shaw (as mentioned in text previously).
> **Unspecified date:** Double deck buses replace single deckers on some limited stop and P (Uppermill circular) services.

As though wartime restrictions were not enough, the weekend of 27/28 January 1940 saw exceptionally severe blizzards which caused further disruption as noted overleaf:

BELOW: Hazards of the blackout. A 1937 Roe-bodied TD5 of the 153-167 batch has had a serious collision with the offside of a lorry, presumably stationary. Note that two of the visible interior lights are without bulbs while the other is masked, as is the nearside headlamp. The distortion of such a major structural feature as the front bulkhead and the obvious effect on two intermediate pillars and the waistrail are evidence of the severity of the impact. *(Courtesy J. J. Holmes)*

Preparation for air raid precautions had begun many months before the war and the blackout was imposed from 1 September 1939. Street obstructions such as lamp posts were at least given white markings. The mudwings, rear panels and some other parts of buses were treated similarly. In Oldham, bus windows were coated internally with blue varnish and, in order to make them less conspicuous from the air, their roofs were painted matt grey. The effect of the window varnish was too drastic during daylight and so it was removed and applied to the interior light bulbs instead. Some buses had anti-blast netting fitted to their windows. Strict regulations governing vehicle lights and speeds were introduced, here condensed:

1 Sep 39:	Side and rear lights to be reduced to an obscured 2-in aperture.
	Lamp reflectors to be blackened.
	Stop lights to be reduced to 1-in opening.
	Number plates and destination indicators not to be illuminated, amended following month to allow partial illumination of destination indicators.
	Direction indicator lights (where fitted) to be reduced to 1-in wide strip.
	Offside headlamp bulb to be removed.
	Nearside headlamp to be masked leaving 2-in aperture, with partial blacking-out of reflector.
22 Jan 40:	Improved form of headlamp mask introduced.
29 Jan 40:	Built-up area speed limit reduced from 30 to 20mph during darkness.
Oct 40	Permissible to use masked headlamp on moving vehicles during air-raid alerts.
	Side light aperture to be reduced to 1in.

These conditions understandably were nerve-wracking for operating staff. In October 1939, Oldham Passenger Transport Committee minuted its praise of bus and tram crews for their care and in the blackout. The Committee also asked intending passengers not to dazzle drivers by shining torches into their eyes. Inevitably, not only were there more collisions during darkness but also more accidents involving pedestrians, some fatal. At the inquest on a Shaw victim in November 1940, the coroner queried whether the bus lights conformed with regulations. It was never established that they did not and a verdict of accidental death was returned. Following many similar fatalities the drivers were exonerated.

In the light of the fuel shortage, the question of alternative propellants came up, as in 1917. During May 1940 it was decided to convert a bus experimentally to run on town gas, diesel-engined 1933 Leyland Tiger 24 being chosen although apparently not until 1941. Again, the gas was stored in a roof-mounted canvas bag which had to be filled two or three times a day at the gasworks. When first started from cold, the engine ran on fuel oil only and then on warming-up, 50 per cent each of fuel oil and gas. The experiment was brought to an abrupt end when a high wind ripped off the gas bag straps. Another perpetual problem, intensified during wartime, was that of exceptional peak demand for transport. Oldham's General Manager, Mr Richards, showed initiative by conferring with employers, employees and others regarding the possibility of staggered working hours at the cotton mills in Shaw. The result was that from 30 December 1940 their starting and finishing times were advanced by 30 minutes and became 7.15am and 5pm respectively, leading to more efficient utilisation of buses at peak periods. As to plans for the future, only days previously the Corporation had placed tentative orders for sixteen Leyland double deck chassis and 21 Daimler single deck, for delivery in 1942/43. By that time, it was calculated, 92 buses would be time expired. They had to keep running. No further new ones were to join the Oldham fleet until 1946.

BELOW: A mishap in Union Street provides the opportunity to illustrate how the wartime grey of Oldham double deck bus roofs was swept down on the rear dome panelling. The bus is 193, a Roe-bodied TD5, its rear panel white marking having become faded and stained. One of the films showing at the Odeon is Tin Pan Alley. *(GMTS)*

LEFT: Gas bag bus, 1941. Roe-bodied Leyland Tiger TS4 No24 was caught on film in a drab setting, displaying the roof-mounted storage bag for its town gas fuel during a short-lived wartime experiment. The pipe from the gas bag to the nearside bulkhead is noteworthy as are the headlamp masks, the sidelight apertures, the blackout markings on the lamp post but not, unusually, on 24's front wings, and the air raid shelter signpost. (*Oldham Evening Chronicle*)

Some months into the war it was realised that as 150 Passenger Transport Department men were liable for military call-up there would be a labour shortage. Initially it was hoped to engage men aged over 42 years as replacements but on 29 May 1940 the Committee decided reluctantly that women would have to be employed as conductresses. The situation was eased a little from 1 February 1941 when bus driving became a reserved occupation, exempting otherwise eligible men from being called up. It is not recorded precisely how many women were employed. The job was intended to be temporary but about 50 of them remained after the war, some for many years (see Chapter I).

During 1940/41, some municipalities such as Birmingham and Coventry suffered devastating bus fleet losses through enemy action. Many other operators then began to disperse their fleets when not in use. Oldham used two locations, one a recreation ground near Rochdale Road which later was to be occupied by the college, the other a coal storage site on Chamber Road, near Ashton Road, owned by the Ministry of Munitions. About 80 buses, mostly those used at peak times only, were parked in the open on these sites between duties and overnight. At that time it was an offence not to immobilise a motor vehicle parked outside and Oldham's method was to remove the steering wheels.

As its vehicle situation was favourable, like some other operators Oldham was able to help some of those with shortages by hiring-out buses. Usually it was older vehicles that were loaned, in Oldham's case Leyland TD2s, TD3s and Crossleys. They went to Bristol Tramways & Carriage, Red & White Motor Services (Chepstow) and Lancashire United (Atherton) for various periods from 3 July 1940 as tabulated in Appendix 3. Red & White was loaned Leylands only, repainting some into its own livery. It wanted to buy

those still on hire in November 1943 but the Committee would not agree to this.

The conservation of fuel and components was an important wartime consideration and in summer 1941, responding to the Commissioner's instructions, Oldham Corporation reduced the number of bus stops. A requirement to cut mileage by a further 10 per cent was imposed on 16 December 1942 in order to conserve more fuel and rubber. The loss of Malaya and other territories to Japan had given the enemy control of 90 per cent of the world's natural rubber resources. So precarious was the situation that the Ministry of Supply would not allow tyres to be renewed unless they were worn completely smooth and almost to the canvas. The service cuts took the form of a curfew when final daily journeys left outer termini between 9.0 and 9.30pm, coupled with the reduction of some frequencies and the withdrawal of services before 2pm on Sundays. There was to be no relaxation until 17 November 1943.

National interest in alternative fuels had begun early in the war and of course Oldham had experimented with town gas on Tiger 24. Following development work, in autumn 1942 the Ministry of War Transport made direct contact with all operators of more than 150 buses, instructing them to convert ten per cent to producer gas operation. In Oldham's case this meant eighteen. Although engine performance was affected adversely, the instruction was given regardless of operating terrain. Operators generally tried to resist it, in part at least, and in fact Oldham converted only four. They were petrol-engined Tigers 63/65 and diesel Titans 80/128. In the case of the Tigers the reduction in performance was offset a little by increasing the cylinder bore of their 6.8-litre engines from 4in to $4^9/_{16}$in, adding some two litres to the total swept volume. The anthracite-fired gas plant was carried on a two-wheel trailer towed by the bus. It needed frequent attention and

OLDHAM CORPORATION PASSENGER TRANSPORT DEPT.

HATHERSHAW–
SUMMIT & ROCHDALE

ALTERATION OF SERVICE

Commencing on Sunday, December 19th, 1943 and until further notice the Service between Hathershaw and Summit will be extended to Rochdale and will operate as follows.

MONDAY TO FRIDAY.

STAR INN TO ROCHDALE: 5-12 a.m., 5-22 a.m. (change at Summit) 5-42 a.m., 6-12 a.m.

HATHERSHAW TO ROCHDALE:

5-44 a.m.,	6-14 a.m.	and every	10	minutes until	8-44 a.m.
	8-59 a.m.	„	15	„ „	11-59 a.m.
	12-4 p.m.	„	10	„ „	1-14 p.m.
	1-29 p.m.	„	15	„ „	4-14 p.m.
	4-24 p.m.	„	10	„ „	6-44 p.m.
	6-59 p.m.	„	15	„ „	9-14 p.m.

SATURDAY.

As Monday to Friday until 6-14 a.m., 6-24 a.m. and every 10 minutes until 9-24 p.m.

SUNDAY.

STAR INN TO ROCHDALE: 1-37 p.m. (change at Summit) 1-52 p.m.

HATHERSHAW TO ROCHDALE: 1-59 p.m. and every 15 minutes until 9-14 p.m.

Buses leaving Rochdale at the hour and 30 minutes past the hour travel through to Ashton.

Buses leaving Rochdale at 10, 20, 40 and 50 minutes past the hour on a 10 minutes service and at 15 and 45 minutes past the hour on a 15 minutes service travel to Hathershaw only.

An intermediate service will operate (Weekdays only) between Hathershaw and Royton as under:—

HATHERSHAW TO ROYTON: 6-49a.m. and every 10 minutes until 8-9 a.m.
ROYTON TO HATHERSHAW: 6-45a.m. „ „ „ „ „ 8-15 a.m.

Wallshaw Depot, Oldham.
December, 1943

A. HENTHORN,
Deputy General Manager.

Wm. Gailey & Son. Printers. 782. Lees Road. Oldham.

emitted an unpleasant, pungent aroma. In order to obviate jack-knifing problems with the trailers, Oldham confined the Tigers to E route (Town Hall - Mossley) and the Titans to 4/V (Circular) or D (Rhodes Bank - Moston Greengate) on which reversing was not necessary at termini. During the eastbound ascent from Lees Brook on the Mossley route one day, the differential casing of Tiger 63 broke and the worm shaft fell out. The driver stopped the bus but then allowed it to run back a little and unfortunately the trailer jack-knifed and was damaged. A more frequent problem was the melting of the trailer casing. There were no regrets when the MoWT allowed producer gas to be abandoned from 12 September 1944. That Oldham originally intended

to convert 18 buses is borne out by the acquisition of 20 trailers 1942, two of them obviously as spares.

The sudden death of Mr J F Richards on 4 October 1943 was a shock to Committee and Department. He was succeeded early in 1944 by Mr Cyril Percy Page from Bury and the post was re-designated General Manager and Engineer. In February 1944, the Oldham, Manchester and Rochdale undertakings acquired for £38,500 the limited-stop Rochdale - Royton - Chadderton - Manchester service operated by Yelloway Motor Services of Rochdale, previously Holt Bros. Of the vehicles included in the transaction, Oldham received a 1938 all-Leyland Titan TD5 which became No227, and two Burlingham-bodied petrol-engined Tiger TS1s which were sold without

LEFT: Joining the fleet in 1944 as the Corporation's share of Yelloway stage carriage vehicles was this 1938 all-Leyland TD5, becoming Oldham 227 (DDK 256). Although plans were made to convert the destination layout to Oldham standard, the work was never carried out and the bus remained odd in this respect until withdrawal in 1952. (Ribble Enthusiasts' Club)

LEFT: "The war is now over," the BBC radio news reader had said and Chas H Roe's eventual response was this elegant development of its pre-war double deck outline after about four years of so-called wartime utility designs, not seen in the Oldham fleet. Wearing a garb of red instead of the usual crimson lake, Oldham's 235 (DBU 27), with painted radiator shell, sunbathes before delivery in 1946. Thicker window pillars and top-sliding vents were post-war developments. The chassis was a Leyland Titan, the TD series having ended in favour of a new one starting at PD1. Oldham took delivery of fourteen—228–241 (R. Marshall)

being operated by Oldham. 227 had semi-coach seats downstairs but otherwise was generally similar to 174-179 in the fleet. The service, numbered 24, was run jointly by the three operators concerned.

The war showed that buses could last for much longer than the common pre-war seven-year span based on the maximum loan period. In 1945, Oldham's oldest vehicles were the 1931 Tiger TS3s, 59-62, but the immediate post-war boom in passenger traffic prevented any withdrawals. Every operator clamoured for new buses but even Leyland Motors needed time to convert to a peacetime footing. Extant orders from Oldham were modified when MoWT licences for new buses were no longer needed. The Leylands and Daimlers ordered in 1942 were eventually merged with the buses of subsequent orders, totalling 134 in 1946, and appeared in various long-awaited post-war deliveries.

First arrivals came in July/October 1946 (228-241) and continued the favourite pre-war theme, teak-framed Roe bodywork on Leyland chassis. The chassis was of the new Titan PD1 model which had only the front axle in common with Leyland's final pre-war Titan design. Power came from a new type of engine, the E181, a 7.4-litre unit with push-rod operated valves and a toroidal combustion chamber. Unlike the pre-war 8.6-litre engine, it emitted a harsh knock. The constant-mesh gearbox was also of a new design and like the pre-war one required skilful handling. 228-241 lacked pre-war comforts such as saloon heating,

1941. Pre-war standard Oldham ventilation had been half-drop windows but from now on it was top-sliding vents.

By 1946, the Passenger Transport Department was eager to restore pre-war service levels and to replace the remaining tram route. The last tram ran on 3 August and the buses of Manchester and Oldham Corporations commenced the replacing 98 bus service, Waterhead – Manchester (Stevenson Square), the following day, with Waterhead - Hollinwood via Werneth short workings numbered 1. As to traffic levels, Appendix 3 shows that total annual passenger numbers and traffic revenue had gone up considerably from pre-war years but costs were rising inexorably, too, wages and salaries representing about 57 per cent of revenue spending. Passenger totals would rise to a peak of 87.5 million in 1956 but the average number of passengers per mile had peaked at 15.24 in 1944. Fares remained at their pre-war levels for a few years but new post-war housing in the outer districts of the town lowered the density of the population. This reduced the number of passengers per mile and strained finances further. Further important factors were to be the de-rationing of petrol on 26 May 1950 followed over the years by a continuing rise in car ownership, and the Coronation on 2 June 1953 which boosted television as a form of entertainment with an inevitable effect on people's travel habits.

The two-axle bus gross weight limit had been raised from 10½ to 11 tons in 1941 and then to 12 tons in 1946, allowing for heavier construction. During the war, some 8ft-wide buses and trolleybuses from frustrated export orders had been diverted to home operators with dispensation. Manufacturers and operators were now pressing for the width limit to be increased by six inches to 8ft and this was granted for operation on individual routes approved by the Traffic Commissioners until 1950, when that condition was lifted. Oldham Corporation standardised on the increased width and operated the first 8ft-wide Leyland motor bus, No244, one of fifty Titans (242-291). These also had bodywork by Chas H Roe, this concern being acquired by Park Royal Vehicles in 1947 (see Appendix 3). The Titans were of type PD1/3, the wider version of the PD1. Nos242-266 were delivered during July-September 1947 and 267-291 during May-July 1948, the second batch lacking the usual Roe raised waistrails. Now to be standard, a service number replaced the destination on the offside. Pre-war comforts such as moquette upholstery and saloon heaters were restored, along with the white and crimson lake livery. This was of a slightly deeper shade than in pre-war days although with subsequent deliveries of paint it became a little lighter. While a new or recently-repainted lined-out Oldham bus looked magnificent, the Pennine rain and industrial atmosphere caused the colours to weather badly and for this reason the livery was to be modified in 1966. All the lining-out was one shade of vermilion although the contrasting background colours created the illusion of different shades. The PD1 and PD1/3 Titans lasted an average of 20 years and No246 survived into preservation.

ABOVE: With about 15 years' strenuous service behind it 228, a Leyland Titan PD1, hurries across the Star Inn junction from Union Street West to Union Street, bound for home and followed by tin front Titan 441. Note the advertisement, the absence of lining-out and the deeper crimson lake band at cantrail-level. It will be seen that, for the first few post-war years, the offside destination has been replaced by a service number. *(Copyright holder not known)*

also having leathercloth-upholstered seats. Their livery incorporated a shade that was lighter than the usual crimson lake but was not perpetuated. Radiator shells were painted. Transport staff called these vehicles *utilities* but in fact they were not. The allocation of new buses was still in MoWT hands when they were built but they were of Roe's original design and although perhaps spartan, did not conform to the MoS/MoWT-approved standard wartime specification for new construction introduced in November

UPPER: Oldham was among the few pioneering operators to take vehicles of the newly-permitted width of eight feet. Twenty-five such Roe-bodied Leyland Titans, designated PD1/3, went into service during 1947 and were among the earliest examples nationally (242-266). Another twenty-five followed in 1948 (267-291). Two representatives of the first delivery pause together here at the garage entrance in 1964. Note that 252 (right) has received new fleet number plates but 247 has not. *(The late R. Taylor collection)*

CENTRE: The 1948 delivery of PD1/3s lacked the characteristic raised waistrails to both saloons. 278 takes a breather outside that celebrated local centre for cultural activities, the Lyceum, Union Street, soon after a repaint, omitting lining-out. *(Copyright holder not known)*

LOWER: Close-up of John Holmes's preserved Leyland Titan PD1/3 No246, showing the E181-type 7.4-litre engine surrounded by gleaming chrome and paintwork. *(Author)*

In 1947 there was concern over the condition of the 21 English Electric-bodied TD5s (132-152). Their bodywork had deteriorated seriously and the Department wanted to replace nine of them and have new bodies fitted to the other twelve. Loan sanction difficulties terminated this plan but it was possible to replace eight and rebuild the bodies of the others. These are the details:

Withdrawn 1948: 134/139/141/142/144/145/147/151.
Rebuilt: by Salmesbury Engineering: 132/133/135-138/140;
by Martin Hearn:143/146/148-150;
by OCPTD: 152

As to services, the most notable changes to arrangements during this period were as given below and later developments are outlined in Appendix 1. Limeside was a new housing development on the lower, south-west side of Oldham. Strinesdale, many years later re-named Pennine Meadows, was an estate at an elevated and airy spot on the north-east side opened in 1947. It remained inaccessible to buses for three years because of unsuitable roads. Services C and F were single deck-operated.

The 1948-50 additions to the fleet following the Leyland PD1/3s were complex and are summarised below. All were 56-seat double deckers except the Crossley SD42s which were 32-seat saloons.

1948:	292-301	Crossley SD42/3	Roe
	302-311	Crossley DD42/5	Crossley
	312-321	Daimler CVD6	Roe
	337	Leyland PD2/3	Roe
1949:	322-336	Daimler CVD6	Crossley
1950:	338-361	Leyland PD2/3	Roe
	362-365	Crossley SD42/7	Roe
	366-369	Crossley DD42/8	Crossley

Crossley Motors, from 1946 based at Errwood Park, Stockport, produced smart-looking post-war chassis featuring low bonnet and radiator, powered by a new 8.6-litre engine which had its gestation in late pre-war years. Research done by Michael Eyre reveals that up to prototype-testing stage it incorporated some cylinder head design features originating with the Saurer concern of Switzerland. When in 1945 the Swiss company asked for royalties on

SUMMARY OF CHANGES TO SERVICES 1948-50

To 17 Jul 48
B   Derker - Booth Hill
F   Shaw - Dogford Rd - Royton - Stottfield - Middleton

From 18 Jul 48
11   Derker - Booth Hill - Royton - Stottfield *(short working of 12)*
12   Derker - Booth Hill - Royton - Stottfield - Middleton
B   Middleton Junc Stn - Cow Hill - Belgrave Rd *(new service)*
F   Shore Edge - Shaw - Dogford Rd - Royton

To 11 Mar 50
7   Chadderton (Victoria St) - Higginshaw or Shaw
(short workings of 3/59)

From 12 Mar 50
7   Higginshaw - Werneth - Chapel Rd - Limeside, later co-ordinated with G, which then became: Limeside - Chapel Rd - Werneth - Town Hall - Abbeyhills

To 25 Mar 50
C   Middleton Junc - Rhodes Bank

From 26 Mar 50
C   Middleton Junc - Town Centre - Ripponden Rd - Strinesdale

LEFT: Shore Edge, with a backcloth of Pennine scenery, provides the setting for Roe-bodied Crossley SD42/3 No 297 of the 1948 batch (292-301) towards the end of its working days and with front tyres that would be illegal by later standards. Two young girls in their Sunday best look on with interest. *(J. Fozard)*

ABOVE: Oldham's first all-Crossley products were ten 1948 DD42/5s (302-311) from the manufacturer's new Errwood Park works in Stockport. Here, bedraggled ten-years-old 307 waits at Hollinwood Avenue for A V Roe employees. Unlike some others of the batch, it has not received a crimson lake band at upper saloon cantrail-level and is clearly in need of a repaint. The radiator has the Coptic cross motif and on this occasion at least, Rochdale Corporation has provided a new Weymann-bodied AEC Regent Mark V for the works service. Both buses would proceed to Broadway, a few hundred yards away, to join routes 2 and 24 respectively. *(The late R. Taylor collection)*

production units, Crossley Motors refused to consider payment and changed the design in a hurry. Regrettably the result was an inefficient engine that lacked the reliability and economy of its competitors. In 1948 the control of Crossley Motors passed to AEC, which subsequently came up with a redesigned cylinder head known as the "downdraught" type which was a considerable improvement. Oldham's 1950 Crossleys had the revised version of the engine and also synchromesh gearboxes. The 1948 examples had an easy-to-handle constant-mesh 'box. (Appendix 3 outlines briefly the AEC-Crossley-Roe relationship during the late 1940s).

The metal-framed Crossley body was of distinctive appearance. The bodybuilder's post-war outline was derived from Manchester Corporation's "streamline" specification of 1936 and a notable feature was the up-stepped waistrail

below the rearmost two windows on either side of each saloon. This had a structural function downstairs as it accommodated the long diagonal bracing stays strengthening the area around the rear wheel arches. The corresponding upstairs windows were shaped to match for styling purposes. When new, at upper saloon waistrail level Crossleys 302-311 did not have the usual band of crimson lake although it was applied to the horizontal moulding around that contour and the band was added to some on subsequent repaints. With the low bonnet line, forward visibility for the driver was excellent. An enigma surrounds the chassis designation of 292-301, however. They were 8ft wide and Oldham records quote it as DD42/5. Many accounts of Crossley history state that the DD42/5 was a 7ft 6in-wide model and the DD42/4 was the contemporary 8ft one. By 1965 the body of Crossley saloon 299 had deteriorated badly although

BELOW LEFT: Body swop. The Crossley body of Southport 117 stands alongside the Roe body it will replace on the Crossley chassis of Oldham 299. There is collision damage to the offside corner of the cab of the Southport bus but repair work to this was obviously more viable than remedial work on the Roe body which had deteriorated badly. *(J J Holmes)* **BELOW RIGHT:** Oldham's 1948 Crossley saloon 299 is seen here with the Crossley body transferred from the Southport Crossley. Note that no attempt has been made to adapt the service number aperture to Oldham's standard and the original Coptic cross radiator shell has been replaced by the Crossley name-badge example from the Southport bus. *(R. Marshall)*

the chassis was fit for continued service. The Corporation therefore bought chassis-damaged all-Crossley single decker 117 from Southport Corporation and transferred the body to 299. So good was the condition of the Southport paintwork that Oldham gave it only a partial repaint. The final Crossley chassis and last non-Leyland to remain in service, 368, was to be rescued for preservation in 1968.

It was intended that Crossley should build all the bodies on the 25 Daimler chassis (312-336) but as the Stockport concern could not promise favourable delivery dates an order for ten (312-321) was transferred to Roe. Crossley frequently built bodies on other makes of chassis although Leyland did not. The Roe bodies on the Daimlers were generally similar to those on Leyland PD1/3s 267-291 and the Crossley bodies to those the Crossley DD42/5s. Daimler had developed its own smooth and refined 8.6-litre CD6-type engine from late pre-war years too. In the CV chassis, Daimler's post-war product,

it was initially optional to either Gardner or AEC units and the usual four-speed preselective gearbox was fitted. During the early 1950s, Roe Daimlers 312/313 were repainted experimentally in liveries incorporating crimson lake upperworks relieved only by white window surrounds on 312 and cream ones on 313. In Bolton, Coventry, Edinburgh, Gateshead, Portsmouth, Wigan and elsewhere there were buses with ample proportions in deep red or dark red-brown hues. The experimental layout, however, just did not seem acceptable in Oldham and the Daimlers were given back their standard format only weeks later.

The Leyland PD2/3 model was the wider version of the PD2/1 (of which Oldham had no new examples), introduced in 1947. A new and considerably more powerful design of engine, the 9.8-litre type O/600, was fitted to the PD2 range, coupled with a standard gearbox with synchromesh on all gears save first. Some drivers thought it less easy to

handle than the Crossley synchro 'box. 337, the first of more than 100 PD2 specimens to join the Oldham fleet to 1958, visited Earls Court, London, to be displayed on the Roe stand at the 1948 Commercial Motor Show before being exhibited to Oldhamers on a less cosy vacant plot of land at West Street. Like Roe Daimler 316, Leyland 337 had fluorescent interior lights and no offside service number aperture. The lights were to be altered to standard within a few years. 337 entered service on 2 November 1948,

seventeen months before 338-361 which differed from 337 only in some small details. Among these were crimson lake rather than black wings which were to be standard for several years. With this delivery the post-war fleet renewal programme was virtually complete. All buses pre-dating the 1935 Leyland-bodied TD4s (102-104), and some buses post-dating them, were withdrawn. The fleet had a fairly low average age once again. Most of the PD2s lasted until 1968 and a few served with the SELNEC PTE until 1970.

LEFT: The 14-storey Civic Centre would later be built on the land alongside 362, one of the four Roe-bodied Crossley SD42/7 chassis of 1950 seen working the 'little C' route. The radiator shell looks somewhat tarnished! (R. Marshall)

LOWER LEFT: 368, the third of four 1950 all-Crossley DD42/8 double deckers, shows off its imposing chromium-plated radiator shell as it waits in Clegg Street, though its Crossley name-badge is missing. The War Memorial is in the background, right. Fortunately this bus was to survive in preservation. (J. Fozard)

Festival of Britain year 1951 saw Oldham's fleet at its peak of 240 buses, a figure that remained unchanged until 1957. During 1946-52, a total of 145 new buses had been added to the fleet, 27 more than the number withdrawn. The additions were needed for tramway replacement, services to new housing areas and to cope with the post-war passenger boom. With the fleet renewed, there followed a quiet period.

Not all the post-war buses were superior to their pre-war counterparts. Greater width meant greater weight, increased further by heavier construction of both chassis and body. Double deck unladen weights had increased from less than $6\frac{1}{2}$ tons in 1933 to about $6\frac{3}{4}$ by wartime. The PD1/3s, however, weighed almost $7\frac{1}{2}$ tons unladen and the subsequent Crossleys, Daimlers and Leyland PD2/3s were around the 8-ton mark. With their moderately-powered and noisy engine in a relatively heavy bus with slow gear-change, PD1/3s often struggled to keep time with heavy loads. Few drivers mastered the clutch-stop fast gear-change technique. Neither were the even heavier Crossleys and Daimlers any better, despite their quicker gear-changes. A table comparing the nominal power output to the unladen weight is given below. On the basis shown, borne out by observation, the PD2/3 was clearly the best, followed by the TD5. Bus performance, of course, would vary according to condition and was affected particularly by the speed of gear changes, or the impracticability of changing to a higher gear, when hill-climbing.

Bus type		bhp per cwt of UW
1948/50	Leyland PD2/3/Roe	0.79
1939-41	Leyland TD5/Roe	0.73
1947/48	Leyland PD1/3/Roe	0.67
1948	all-Crossley	0.62
1949	Daimler/Crossley	0.61

Note: these figures are purely theoretical and take no account of hill-climbing ability by reference to gearbox and rear axle ratios.

No more new buses were placed in service until 1952, and then only three Leyland Titan PD2/12s (370-372). This model differed from the PD2/3 only in having the wheelbase lengthened by two inches to 16ft 5in for fitting with 27ft-long bodywork, legalised for two-axle double deckers on 1 June 1950. The bodies were of Leyland's own 'Farington' style, metal-framed, and clearly descended from the ageless late pre-war design. Leyland was to cease bodybuilding in 1954. With 370-372 the practice of displaying the service number on the offside ended. Wings were black again but the upper saloon waistrail band of crimson lake was omitted. When 370-372 were delivered the fleet could be summarised as shown in the accompanying table:

BELOW: The 1952 all-Leyland PD2/12s originally were all white above cantrail-level but a crimson lake band was added later. Middle bus of the trio, 371 (HBU 124) is seen well-laden in Yorkshire Street on its way from Mills Hill to Rushcroft. These were the first new double-deckers to have no offside destination or service number indicator. *(Copyright holder not known)*

OLDHAM CORPORATION
Fleet profile—1952

By age

Type	Year	Number in service
Double deck		
Leyland TD4	1934/35	9
Leyland TD5	1937-41	80
Daimler COG6	1937	6
Leyland PD1	1946	14
Leyland PD1/3	1947/48	50
Leyland PD2/3	1948/50	25
Daimler CVD6	1948/49	25
Crossley DD42/5	1948	10
Crossley DD42/8	1950	4
Leyland PD2/12	1952	3
Double deck total		*226*
Single deck		
Crossley SD42/3	1948	10
Crossley SD42/7	1950	4
Single deck total		*14*

By chassis make

	Number in service
Leyland	181
Daimler	31
Crossley	28
Total	*240*

By body make

Roe	187
English Electric	12
Leyland	12
Crossley	29
Total	*240*

Further housing developments took shape at Fitton Hill on the south side of town near Hathershaw, and at Holts on the east side beyond Abbeyhills. Fitton Hill received a bus service on 16 July 1953 when the B route, Middleton Junction Station - Belgrave Road, was extended into the new estate. A Town Hall - Holts bus service was commenced following Committee approval given on 15 September 1954. To some extent this duplicated the N (Oldham—Stalybridge) and G/7 services (Limeside—Waterloo St—Abbeyhills) and so within a year new arrangements were made. These were the withdrawal of service 20 and the extending of the Limeside services to become:

G   Limeside—Holts; and
7   Holts—Limeside.

The ogre of rising costs was continuing to harass operators. That important figure, average working expenses per mile expressed as a percentage of traffic revenue, had been as low as a comforting 68 for Oldham in 1937. It reached 86 in 1950 and was set to remain typically at about 93 during the 1950s/60s, peaking at an alarming 99 in 1958 before falling a little again. In 1947, Mr Paige had warned of a difficult future. It had arrived now in the form of rapidly rising costs of labour, materials and fuels. As at 17 March 1954 fuel oil was about 3s 8½d (18.54p) per gallon to the transport industry but a constant irritation was the high level of taxation included. This was 2s 6d (12.5p) and had contributed to a price rise of 45 per cent in three years and 250 per cent from pre-war. Operators lobbied but to no avail. Although not a major cost it was a

BELOW: Fourth of the five tin front Leyland Titan PD2/20 chassis with Metro-Cammell Orion bodies, placed in service on 1 January 1955, 376 (KBU 386) is seen in Oldham's King Street on the Rochdale - Ashton service. The dirty streaks are inexcusable and it will be understood how the body proportions gave rise to the derogatory 'loaf tin' epithet. An appearance of gauntness is created by the depth of the upper saloon front panel, made narrower by the tapering of the body in plan view to the width of the tin front. *(J. Fozard)*

significant one. In Oldham, employees' pay now represented about 65 per cent of working expenses and fuel oil about 12 per cent.

One method of increasing revenue, although only by a relatively small amount, was to carry external advertisements on the buses. Oldham accepted its first contract on 18 November 1953. It was usually reckoned also that a saving of about one mile per gallon could made by reducing the unladen weight of a bus by one ton. Several coachbuilders, notably Harrington's of Hove in 1945, used wartime aircraft-production experience to save weight with aluminium alloy-framed PSV bodies. Others such as Saunders-Roe and Scottish Aviation later did likewise but the technique did not gain wide acceptance. By 1952, however, manufacturers were beginning to respond to the cry for fuel-saving buses and the Metropolitan-Cammell-Weymann (MCW) organisation displayed a double deck body on a Daimler chassis at the Show that year, the complete vehicle weighing only 6ton 2cwt unladen. This was achieved by paring down the body structure and fittings as far as practicable, using steel for the main framework members with aluminium alloy elsewhere. The chassis was also of lighter construction. MCW's patented five-bay design, produced independently by Metro-Cammell and by Weymann's, was type-named "Orion" (see Appendix 3 concerning the relationship between these builders). Generally, future vehicles fitted with it were not so light as the 1952 Show bus.

Oldham ordered fifteen Leyland chassis late in October 1953, ten to be Roe-bodied. The rest were to have Orion bodies, the order being placed only after the cautious Committee had visited the Metro-Cammell works to in-

spect examples. The Titan chassis was the new PD2/20 type which was technically similar to the PD2/12 but incorporated a wider bonnet and concealed radiator arrangement that became known as the "tin front", replacing the traditional exposed radiator shell. Other chassis-builders were marketing their own versions although they had been around for several years, notably with Birmingham Corporation and the Midland Red company and on Foden post-war forward-engined bus chassis.

The Roe-bodied batch arrived first, in September 1954 (378-387). Built to the expected high standard and of course teak-framed, their outline was derived from Roe's majestic "Pullman" design, in this case four-bay. They were by no means lightweights, being only 1½cwt less than Roe-bodied 337-361 of 1948/50 which were one foot shorter. The deeper windows added a little to the weight but a small amount was saved by the use of some lighter materials such as pressed aluminium interior window finishers (now to be a standard Roe feature for Oldham although not always of the same design).

The Orion-bodied five, 373-377, entered service on 1 January 1955. Their unladen weight was practically down to seven tons and it showed. Versions elsewhere, however, weighed less than 6¾ tons. Oldham's examples lacked interior lining panels and this, with the standard frameless front and rear upper saloon roof domes, helped to make them hot in summer and cold in winter, despite heaters. They had no interior window finishers, and no vertical beadings between the exterior panels although the Corporation added these later. The crimson lake band at upper saloon waistrail level was omitted, too, although at least

BELOW: Ten of the fifteen PD2/20 chassis ordered for 1954 delivery were bodied by Roe (378-387) to 'Pullman'-derived outline with deep windows. Stevenson Square in Manchester is the setting for 385 (KBU 380), the evening sunshine highlighting its stately features as it stands in the company of a Manchester all-Crossley bus of the 1947/48 period. Although, like the Orion, the Roe body also tapered in at the front, the appearance was not affected adversely. Note the crude wartime corrugated iron-roofed shelter, proof only against vertical rain! (J. Fozard)

some had it added upon repainting. Despite the special springs offered by Leyland for lightweight-bodied Titans they bounced uncomfortably on an uneven surface, particularly when lightly-loaded. These buses quickly earned the nickname "loaf tins" in Oldham. A Yorkshire journalist called Orions "tin boxes" and "cans". An Edinburgh dignitary used the now-famous lyricism, "ungainly, inelegant, monstrous masses of shivering tin", and an eminent municipal general manager said they were the bodies on which it continued raining inside after the rain had stopped outside.

An additional anxiety for many operators at this time and in the future was shortage of hourly-paid staff. With plentiful other employment offering comparable pay without shift and weekend work, the transport industry had problems recruiting and keeping personnel. As at 20 October 1954, Oldham was short of about 15 per cent of platform staff and more than 20 per cent of cleaners. The situation was alleviated a little by the decision in December 1954 to install a Dawson bus washing machine in the garage.

Leylands 373-387 replaced the three all-Leyland TD4s and the remaining twelve English Electric-bodied TD5s.

There were still 74 Leylands and six Daimlers of pre-war years left and in order to replace some of these, 31 new Leyland chassis were ordered early in 1955, bodywork orders going to Roe for twenty, Park Royal Vehicles for five and Northern Counties Motor & Engineering of Wigan for six. The Park Royal order was fulfilled by the subsidiary Crossley concern which although no longer producing chassis was still active in bodybuilding. The following year, so as to clear out the rest of the pre-war stock, 44 more Leylands were ordered with 24 of the bodies from Roe and ten each from Northern Counties and Metro-Cammell. In the interests of more efficient vehicle-usage, seating capacities were increased from the previous standard of 56, although there were variations. The following table summarises the deliveries:

1957	388-407	Leyland PD2/20	Roe 60-seat
	408-412	Leyland PD2/20	Crossley 61-seat
	413-418	Leyland PD2/20	NCME 61-seat
1958/59	419-428	Leyland PD2/30	Metro-Cammell 65-seat
1958	429-452	Leyland PD2/30	Roe 65-seat
1958/59	453-462	Leyland PD2/30	NCME 65-seat

RIGHT: The bodywork order for a further 31 Leyland PD2/20 chassis delivered in 1957 was split three ways with Roe building twenty 60-seaters (388-407). This interior view of 388's upper saloon shows the aluminium window pressings with chromatic grey finish, standard from the 1954 Roe delivery. The upper saloon is aluminium alloy-framed with panels and beadings riveted in position and not screwed. *(J. J. Holmes)*

LOWER RIGHT: The third coachbuilder producing bodywork for the 1957 PD2/20 chassis was Northern Counties of Wigan. There were six examples (413-418), all with 61 seats, and in this scene 414 gets the green at the Star Inn on King Street. In later years, the half-drop windows were replaced by top-sliding vents and 414 also lost its upper saloon front vents in favour of fixed panes. *(Copyright holder not known)*

A variation to the transmission was introduced with the 1957 Leylands, the gearbox now having no synchromesh on second as well as first gear. The PD2/30 chassis differed only in minor details from the PD2/20. None of these buses were lightweight. All weighed around 7¾ tons except the Crossley-bodied five which were just less than 7½. The bodies of 419-428 were Orions, five-bay again unlike the

nounced and 388-407 were delivered without lining-out. It was not to be abandoned just yet, though. The Roe 65-seaters had a modified staircase of 3-4-1 layout rather than 2-5-1 and the stair window was omitted. As the top of the forward-ascending stairs was positioned 10in more rearward than previously, the intrusion of the staircase into the lower saloon was eliminated and this provided additional

LEFT: Forty-four PD2/30 chassis were ordered for 1958 delivery, the first ten numerically (419-428) having Metro-Cammell Orion bodies that were of heavier construction and generally better-appointed than the earlier lightweight specimens, except for the reduced number of window vents. 422 is seen here displaying its replacement 'tin' front of glass fibre-reinforced plastics while laying over near Yelloway's Rochdale premises before a limited-stop run to Manchester. *(J. Fozard)*

LOWER LEFT: Star Inn corner is the scene here for 411, fourth of the five Crossley-bodied 1957 Leyland PD2/20s, crossing from Union Street to Union Street West as a Foden eight-wheeler turns into king Street. The 61-seat bodywork bears some resemblance to that of its cousin, the London Transport Routemaster, built by Park Royal, this concern being related to Crossley within the ACV Group. It will be observed that, unlike Metro-Cammell, the Northern Counties and Roe products, in plan view the front of the Crossley bodies did not taper inward to the width of the Leyland tin-front. As to durability, the 1957 Crossley bodies were to prove inferior to earlier ones of that make in Oldham's fleet. *(Copyright holder not known)*

other bodies, but of a more substantial build than the previous Metro-Cammell delivery. Interior lining panels and pressed aluminium window finishers were included. Roe standard construction now incorporated teak framing for the lower saloon and aluminium alloy for the upper, some of the weight saved being offset by the greater number of seats. Northern Counties and Crossley also used aluminium alloy for the upper saloon framing with steel for the lower. The frontal rake of the Roe bodies was less pro-

space for seating on both decks. The Crossley bodies were of Park Royal outline with some family likeness to the London Transport Routemaster which was then being developed and in which Park Royal had major involvement. Oldham found these bodies disappointing. In later years they needed expensive remedial work which only 409 received. The other four, although passing to SELNEC in 1969, were out of use by then and withdrawn in 1970. 409 carried on until 1973.

ABOVE: Two dozen of the 1958 Titans, which were of type PD2/30, bore Roe bodywork of the usual elegant style. This Market Place study of 452 (PBU 952) illustrates how the lining-out, although adding to painting costs, improved an otherwise unexciting tin front, assisted perhaps by the Leyland winged badge. All the PD2/30s were 65-seaters. *(Copyright holder not known)*

BELOW: The final ten PD2/30s numerically (453-462) received Northern Counties bodywork. 460 here corners at the Market Place in company with a Humber Hawk and a Morris Minor. *(Copyright holder not known)*

Some of the tin-front Titans were involved in spectacular accidents during their careers. When only weeks old, Northern Counties-bodied 418 beheaded itself under a low bridge in Rochdale while on a diversion. Severe frontal damage was sustained by another three. Orion-bodied 377 collided with a lamp post in Henshaw Street. Roe-bodied 439 tried to enter a house while descending Manchester Road, and Orion-bodied 424 rammed a van at the Rochdale Road/Barker Street junction.

On 1 July 1956 the maximum length for two-axle double deckers was increased from 27 to 30ft. Few operators seized the opportunity here and Oldham was not to obtain any 'deckers of the new length until 1964. However, a 30ft-long double deck demonstrator that was touring the country visited the town for a week in April 1959. This was an AEC-Park Royal Bridgemaster B3RA, registered 116 TMD, of integral (that is, chassisless) construction and low-height design (13ft 6in rather than 14ft 6in) but with normal seating on both decks. Oldham had no need of low-height buses and it may have been interest in the very bouncy coil-spring suspension, or the 9.6-litre AEC type AV590 engine that prompted the venture. In any event, no AECs or low height or coil-sprung buses were ever acquired.

That period around 1960 was a further stable if uneventful one for Oldham's fleet of 235 buses, the oldest of which were the 1946 Leylands. The fleet age profile was rising, though, for only 101 vehicles (43 per cent) dated from after 1950. Oldham's tin-front Titan era was over and future deliveries were to be significantly different both in appearance and mechanical specification. Moreover, the undertaking was entering its final decade.

RATIONALISATION OF SERVICES BETWEEN MARKET PLACE AND MOORSIDE AS IMPLEMENTED IN 1957

The old and new arrangements are shown for comparison:

Old route		New route	
C*	Middleton Jc - Market Pl - Moorside - Strinesdale	C*	Middleton Jc - Market Pl - Bar Gap Rd
H	Market Pl - Moorside - Grains Bar - Denshaw	H	*Withdrawn*
5**	Westhulme Av - Market Pl - Moorside - Grains Bar	5**	Westhulme Av - Market Pl - Moorside - Strinesdale
6**	Chadderton (Burnley La) - Market Pl - Moorside	6**	Chadderton (Burnley La) - Market Pl - Moorside - Grains Bar - Denshaw

* Single deck-operated

**Co-ordinated, Westhulme Av - Moorside

Further service revisions took place in 1959, affecting Holts as follows:

To 18 Apr 59		From 19 Apr 59	
7	Holts - Limeside (Laburnum Rd) *(one direction)*	7	Abbeyhills - Limeside (Laburnum Rd) *(one direction)*
G	*Converse of 7*	G	*Converse of 7*
4	Town Hall - Glodwick Rd - Park Rd - Tn Hall (Circular)	4	Holts - Park Rd - Tn Hall - Glodwick Rd - Holts (circular route)
V	*Converse of 4*	V	*Converse of 4*

G

Early in 1961, Mr C P Paige announced that he would be retiring from his post as General Manager and Engineer in July, although he did remain until 30 September. The following day he was succeeded by the man who had been his deputy since the end of 1959 and previously Technical Superintendent of Liverpool Corporation Transport, Mr Harry Taylor.

In a report on bus replacement dated 15 November 1961, requested by the Committee, Mr Taylor stated that previously, Oldham had bought buses in sizeable quantities irregularly. This created peaks and troughs of work as relatively large numbers were due for repainting, overhaul and eventually withdrawal at the same time. Mr Taylor recommended the replacing of thirteen buses per year, enabling the then current fleet of 235 to be renewed in 18 years. For a start, he suggested the ordering of 39 buses for delivery over a three-year period ending 31 March 1964.

The Committee had already agreed to the transfer of £15,000 a year to the reserve fund for bus replacement and the balance then stood at £44,500. Mr Taylor said it was desirable to buy new buses out of revenue in order to reduce the burden of loan charges. He pointed out, however, that the suggested programme would cost £85,000 a year and while the first 13 buses could be bought from revenue, borrowing would be necessary for future purchases. In conclusion, he urged that three new types of bus should be hired for evaluation. The Committee agreed to spend £500 on this (see table below) and in principle accepted the General Manager's other proposals. In 1967 the fleet renewal span was to be reduced from 18 to 16 years.

Leyland's Titan PD3, introduced in 1956, was a lengthened version of the PD2 with generally similar options of transmission, brakes and frontal arrangements, suitable for bodywork with entrance in a rear or forward position. The rear-engined Atlantean with set-back front axle, however, was a front-entrance bus, marketed from 1958 although most operators were in no rush to buy it immediately. "Pneumo-cyclic" was the name given to Leyland's semi-automatic, direct-acting epicyclic gearbox. With this, transmission was through a centrifugal clutch (subsequently replaced by a fluid-friction clutch, comprising a fluid flywheel for smoother starting and a centrifugal clutch that engaged automatically as engine speed rose, giving a more "solid" drive). Only accelerator and brake pedals were needed. The visitors ran in normal service and useful data was collected. On 18 July 1962, the Committee inspected all three and the decided to order 26 large-capacity for-

ward-entrance double deckers for delivery equally in 1964/65, later amended to 20 double deck and six single deck. These last-mentioned were intended for driver-only operation which was allowed only on single deckers. Oldham had given it up in 1926!

In the meantime, the Committee had been approached by Seddon Diesel Vehicles Ltd whose premises were at Heyside, between Oldham and Shaw. Their workers were on short time: could they expect business from the Corporation? The reply was that they could tender, but at that time Seddon did not produce the type of vehicles required by the Passenger Transport Department. However, when an AEC Matador lorry chassis was acquired in 1963 as the basis of a new breakdown tender, it proved impracticable for the Department's own workshop to build the body and the work was given to Pennine Coachcraft, a subsidiary of Seddon.

A further new housing development at Alt, immediately south of Abbeyhills, was taking shape. On 18 July 1962 the Committee approved a change to the Holts - Town Hall 4/V services and the 4 became Town Hall - Abbeyhills - Alt - Holts. Further service revisions took place the following year as noted here:

To 21 Sep 63	
A	Chapel Rd - Coppice - Star Inn - Greenacres
H	*letter out of use since 1957*
B	Middleton Junc Stn - Fitton Hill
C	Middleton Junc - Market Pl - Bar Gap Rd
G*	Limeside - Chapel Rd - Werneth - Town Hall - Waterloo St - Abbeyhills
7*	Abbeyhills - Limeside (converse of G)
5+	Strinesdale - Chadderton (Burnley Lane)
6+	Denshaw - Chadderton (Burnley Lane)

One direction only

From 22 Sep 63	
A+	Limeside - Chapel Rd - Coppice - Star Inn - Greenacres
H+	Limeside - Heron St - Coppice - Star Inn - Greenacres
B	Extended at Fitton Hill (Fir Tree Av - Secondary School)
C	Middleton Junc - Market Pl - Egerton St - Higginshaw
G♦	Town Hall - Waterloo St - Abbeyhills (one early morning journey extended to Holts; from 1966 other journeys extended from Abbeyhills to south end of Alt La)
7♦	Limeside - Chapel Rd - Werneth - Market Pl - Bar Gap Rd
5+	Extended at Chadderton (Burnley La - Chadderton Hall Park)
6+	Extended as 5
	♦ Both directions + Co-ordinated service

There were two more bus borrowings in 1963. One involved single deck Manchester Corporation 59, a 1962 Leyland Tiger Cub PSUC1/12, with the engine mounted horizontally amidships under the floor. This example had a Park Royal 38-seat dual-purpose body (that is, suitable for bus and some forms of coach duty) in the two-tone blue

---

July 1962 saw the following three buses, all 30ft-long and 8ft-wide Leyland double deckers with forward- or front-entrance bodies, borrowed from neighbouring municipalities for assessment:

Operator & No	:	Manchester 3621 (UNB 621)	Huddersfield 406 (UCX 406)	Halifax 206 (KCP 15)
Year & type	:	1959 Atlantean PDR1 /1	1961 Titan PD3A/2	1959 Titan PD3/4
Body & type code	:	Metro-Cammell H44/33F	Roe H39/31F	Metro-Cammell H42/30F
Engine & position	:	O.600, transverse rear	O.600, conventional forward	O.600, conventional forward
Gearbox	:	4-speed Pneumo-cyclic	4-speed Pneumo-cyclic	4-speed synchromesh
Bonnet, etc	:	rear 'bustle'	glass fibre wide front, concealed radiator	traditional bonnet, exposed radiator shell

TOP LEFT: Titan on trial – 1. Huddersfield Corporation 406, a PD3A/2 with Roe forward-entrance body and striking red and cream livery style, was hired for evaluation during the summer of 1962 and is seen taking a short break at Hollinwood station. *(The late R. Taylor collection)*

CENTRE: Titan on trial – 2. A Metro-Cammell forward entrance body was fitted to Halifax 206, a PD3/4 hired at the same time and pictured here in its orange, green and cream livery at Shaw. *(The late R. Taylor collection)*

BOTTOM: Atlantean on trial – 1. Manchester 3621, a Metro-Cammell-bodied PDR1/1 chassis, is caught here at Burnley Lane while being tested in July 1962. The bland body style is matched by a dull livery of red with just one relieving band at cantrail level. Note the 'Strinesdale' board in the nearside front window. *(J. J. Holmes)*

UPPER RIGHT: Tiger Cub on trial. Wearing the airport service livery of two-tone blue with dividing waistrail silver band, Manchester's 59, a PSUC1/12 chassis with Park Royal dual doorway, dual purpose body reposes in Oldham garage while in loan in 1963. An order for Tiger Cubs followed the tests.
(J.J.Holmes)

RIGHT: Atlantean on trial - 2. Although also a Metro-Cammell product, the body styling of Liverpool Atlantean L623 contrasts with that of the Manchester vehicle. Borrowed in December 1963, the Merseyside bus is caught by the winter sun in this picture on company with Oldham Leyland PD2/20 No401. Future Oldham vehicle policy was influenced by experience of L623 and Atlanteans were later placed in service, although not with Metro-Cammell bodies.
(J. J. Holmes)

livery of the Airport Service. Borrowed for two weeks, it had a front entrance and centre exit which, on a vehicle operated with driver only, helped to speed up loading and unloading. This trial was to result in an order for Tiger Cubs. The other vehicle borrowed was a new Leyland Atlantean PDR1/1 Mark II, Liverpool Corporation's number L623. This undertaking was setting a new trend. Many body designs for rear-engined double deckers had come to be regarded by some as ungainly and uninspiring, characterised by several of the crude features introduced with certain lightweight types from 1952. A few operators were to specify imaginative and well-proportioned outlines. Nota-

ble among them was Liverpool and from 1962, Metro-Cammell built many bodies to the city's design stipulations. Details included equal-depth windows to both saloons, peaked roof domes at front and rear, a raised floor-level in the lower saloon and a pair of back-to-back double transverse seats over rear wheelarch. L623 ran in Oldham for a few weeks and made a favourable impression. Mr Taylor told reporters, "I think this is the vehicle of the future." Certainly, a variation of it was to become Oldham's standard double deck bus.

During the 1960s, the appearance of the fleet underwent some changes at Mr Taylor's instigation. There had been a

ABOVE: Colour experiment–1. Posed at Alexandra Park, Roe-bodied Leyland PD2/20 No 402 was chosen for a livery trial in 1963. The trial two-tone blue layout with yellow relief may be compared with the traditional livery—now unlined—as worn by PD2/30, No 461. (J. J. Holmes)

LEFT: Colour experiment–2. Within weeks, 402 was modified as shown here at Greenacres Cemetery. The band at cantrail level is white. (J. J. Holmes)

minor livery change from 1957, when the vermilion lining-out first began to be left off. Mr Taylor gave instructions for the omitting of the white band below the lower saloon raised waistrail on Roe bodies, a minor cost-saving measure. More radically, though, in September 1963 with Committee approval the colours and layout were changed experimentally on 1957 Roe-bodied Leyland 402, as follows:

Roof to bottom of lower saloon windows: peacock blue.

Lower saloon panels, tin front, bonnet area: garter blue, extended within a few weeks to top of lower saloon windows.

Lower saloon raised waistrail: yellow , repainted garter blue when that colour extended.

Cantrail-level band: peacock blue at first but white when modifications carried out.

Public reaction was adverse and although no more buses were treated similarly, 402 had the blues until 1966. Other municipal operators ran buses in mostly-blue liveries of various shades, including neighbouring Ashton-under-Lyne, and Birkenhead, Bradford, Leigh, Hull, Middlesbrough, South Shields and Walsall, for example, but as with the crimson lake experiments in the early 1950s, the change did not seem in keeping with expectations. Weathering problems with the traditional colours persisted, however. The search for something different ended in February 1966 when two further new colours were adopted. Crimson lake and white were replaced by pommard and Devon cream respectively which, while different, were not so far removed from the old colours as to create an outcry. Pommard was a deep pink, taking its name from the home of a Burgundy wine, and although the colour did not deteriorate with the ravages of weather and detergent, the paint did assume a somewhat dull finish after some months. The new colours were applied in the same proportions as the old ones except that the cantrail-level band in the darker colour was omitted. The coat-of-arms on each side was moved from the lower saloon panelling to the foremost upper saloon side panel, accompanied by the title "County Borough of Oldham". Previously this had not been displayed but "Oldham Corporation" appeared internally at the front of both saloons.

Another of Mr Taylor's innovations was the introduction in 1962 of metal fleet number plates in place of the traditional serified tramway-style characters, applied by transfer. The plates were similar to those used by some British Transport Commission companies such as Bristol, Western National, Crosville and others and, in a larger size, by Liverpool Corporation, Mr Taylor's previous employer. Daimler 325 and Leylands 394-396 were among the first Oldham buses to carry them, situated at front and rear, and above the foremost lower saloon window on each side. A smaller version was positioned over the fuel filler.

One further innovation affected only the tin-front Leyland Titans. The centre slotted radiator grille panel was replaced by a glass fibre-reinforced plastics one with slightly different slots, produced in the bus garage workshops. It was probably neater than the original which owed its origin to a 1952 Midland Red specification. When the new grille panels were fitted in Oldham, new metal outer panels to the tin front were put on also, incorporating Leyland's alternative style and position of sidelights. These were round rather than bullet-shaped and situated about a foot higher. From 1968 a successful replica of the whole tin frontal assembly was produced from plastics in Oldham, in a manner similar to that undertaken in Edinburgh, replacing thc original version.

By the early 1960s, it was becoming difficult and expensive to obtain spare parts for some early post-war buses. Such engines as those in Oldham's Crossleys, Daimlers and Leyland PD1s and PD1/3s had long been out of production and in 1962, ACV Sales ceased supplying *all* Crossley components. Oldham alleviated the position by acquiring these old buses to be dismantled for parts:

Date	Qty	Chassis	Body	Year(s) new	Acquired from	Original Fleet Nos
1962	2	Crossley DD42/7S	Crossley	1948/49	Liverpool CT	C626/C632
1964	6	Daimler CVD6*	Metro-Cammell	1948/49	Birmingham CT	1841/1843/1956/ 1961/1965/1966
1964	2	Leyland PD1	Weymann	1949	Bury CT	134/147

*The chromium-plated radiator shells and also the Daimler engines from these buses were transferred to Oldham's Roe-bodied 312 and Crossley-bodied 324-326/329/330

BELOW: Make sure it's right, lads! Fitters make final adjustments to Daimler 312 after installing an ex-Birmingham Daimler engine and transferring the chromium-plated radiator shell. *(J J Holmes)*

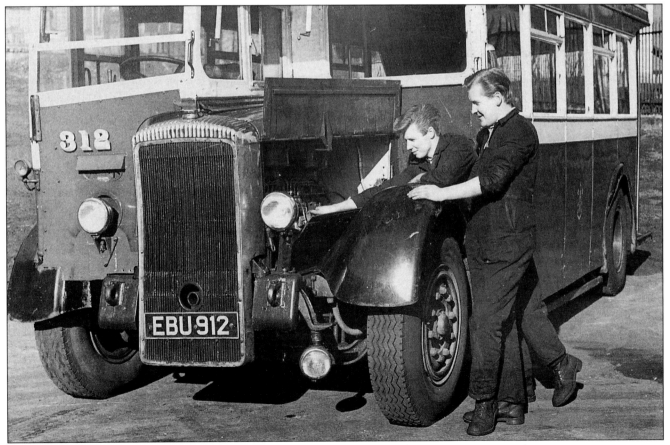

ABOVE: Oldham's biggest buses since the six-wheel era arrived in 1964 in the shape of ten 30ft-long Leyland Titan PD3/5 chassis with 73-seat bodywork of Chas H Roe's usual handsome outline. A new numerical sequence was commenced at 101 and the bus shown here on public display before entry into service is 103. The choice of forward-entrance bodywork with exposed radiator was perhaps surprising for Oldham in view of the number of tin front Titans in the fleet. In one large frontal aperture five separate blinds were now used to convey route and destination details. *(Oldham Evening Chronicle)*

Oldham's first new buses since 1958, ten 73-seat Roe-bodied Leyland Titan PD3/5s, were delivered during April/May 1964 and commenced a new fleet-numbering series as 101-110. Recalling the 1962 trials and their outcome, they featured a mixture of Halifax and Huddersfield specifications and were the first ten buses of the ensuing order. Although they had the well-established 9.8-litre Leyland O/600 engine and reverted to the traditional exposed radiator shell, they broke new ground in being 30ft long, having a forward entrance and Pneumo-cyclic gearbox. Interior lining and ceiling panels and window finishers were of laminated plastics. Lighting was fluorescent, now to be standard for new fleet additions. The roof incorporated two panels of white opaque perspex. At the front, a much enlarged aperture embracing destination and route blinds and a three-track service number blind was featured, the destination also being shown above the foremost nearside window and the service number at the rear. With the usual Roe teak and aluminium alloy framing, the unladen weight was nearly 8¾ tons. Oldham's future new bodies were to be steel-framed and although existing PD-series buses in the fleet were vacuum-braked, air-pressure brakes were standard with the Pneumo-'box and both were to feature in subsequent deliveries.

The first of the PD3s to be delivered was 103 and it was displayed in the town centre. When all ten arrived they were used principally on the busy and co-ordinated O/T services, Hollinwood - Lees (County End or Stamford Road) or Grotton respectively. Regrettably they soon fell from favour with some people. Drivers castigated them as poor pullers and said they suffered from fluid-friction clutch-slip. Conductors complained of having nowhere to stand clear of passenger movement and of needing to go upstairs to change the front blinds, either disturbing seated passengers or being trapped in the rush of those boarding at termini. Everyone was almost deafened by the squealing of the brakes. One bus, 108, was scrapped after it collided with a tanker and overturned, injuring 46 passengers, at the Rochdale Road/West Street junction on 3 November 1968. The others were withdrawn by the PTE after only 13 years' service, five years short of the original Oldham plan.

At the time the PD3s were new, there was concern about the condition of the Crossley saloons. Although there were six new single deckers on order, the General Manager was authorised to spend up to £3,500 on buying four suitable second-hand saloons. However, none could be found. The situation was alleviated a little by the delivery in summer 1964 of the first four 30ft-long Leyland Tiger

FROM THE INSIDE: PD3/5 No107 showing forward and rearward views of the lower and upper saloons and the entrance platform and doors as seen from the top of the stairs. Note the extensive use of plastics for panelling, the fluorescent lighting and the differences in upholstery. It will be appreciated why conductors complained of having nowhere to stand conveniently!

Views:

A	lower saloon, forward view;	A	B
B	lower saloon, rearward view;	C	D
C	upper saloon, forward view;		
D	upper saloon, rearward view;	E	
E	platform, reflected from top of stairs.		

(All: J. J. Holmes)

Cubs, 111-114, of type PSUC1/13 with 6.5-litre O.400 engine. Leyland had introduced the Tiger Cub as a lightweight model in 1952, improving it in stages over the years. The 41-seat bodywork had front entrance and centre exit, which were to be standard on Oldham's future saloons, and was built by Marshall of Cambridge. This concern had started in coachbuilding as recently as 1959 after taking over Mulliner's of Birmingham. Its origins lay in the motor trade and aviation, however, and it had carried out some body rebuilding for London Transport soon after the war. Marshall won orders from a range of operators, including others from Oldham.

The interior detail of 111-114 was designed by 21-year-old Geoffrey Hampson of the Borough Architect's Department, to which Mr Taylor had referred the matter. Again, extensive use was made of laminated plastics materials. Features included luggage racks, a pram pen and two opening perspex roof lights. The front destination arrangement was a smaller version of that seen on PD3s 101-110. Tiger Cub 111 ventured abroad when new in July 1964, taking a party of local young people on a youth exchange visit to Oldham's twin town, Kranj (pronounced *Kraun-ya*) in the former Yugoslavia. For a time the bus was named *Kranj* in commemoration of its 2,600-mile return trip. In August 1964, similar bus 113 became a star when it featured in some television drama moorland location scenes beyond Denshaw with Driver Harry Weems at the wheel. All four Tiger Cubs were in service by September and as at

that time Oldham had no agreement to run driver-only services, they were crew-operated until August 1966.

The other two saloons, 115/116, had bodywork of similar layout built by local concern Pennine Coachcraft, arriving in February/March 1965. They were a little heavy at nearly 7¼ tons, almost half a ton more than 111-114 and possibly among the heaviest of British Tiger Cub buses. Pennine Coachcraft, incidentally, was to build single deck bodies for other municipalities including Eastbourne, Great Yarmouth, Halifax, Morecambe & Heysham, Warrington, Portsmouth, Reading, Rochdale, Swindon and Todmorden. From 1970, marketing was done under the Seddon name (as before 1964) but production ended in 1974.

In more than one sense, 1965 was a memorable year. On the positive side, May/June saw the delivery of the town's first Leyland Atlanteans which completed the order dating back to 1962. Like other Atlanteans delivered to 1968, they had 77-seat single-doorway bodies, built in this case by Roe. Subsequent Atlanteans had centre exits and 74 seats. New deliveries from 1965 are outlined in the table below:

1965	121-130	Leyland Atlantean	Roe
1966	131-135	Leyland Atlantean	East Lancs*
	136-147	Leyland Atlantean	Roe*
1967	148-152	Leyland Atlantean	Neepsend
	153-160	Leyland Atlantean	Roe
	117-120	Leyland Panther Cub	Marshall
1967/68	161-171	Leyland Atlantean	Roe
1968	172-177	Leyland Panther	Marshall
1969	178-182	Leyland Atlantean	Roe
1970♦	183-187+	Leyland Atlantean	Roe
1971♦	188-199+	Leyland Atlantean	Roe

* 131-147 introduced the revised livery of pommard and cream
+ Intended OCPTD fleet numbers. Were SELNEC 5183-5199
♦ Ordered by OCPTD but delivered to SELNEC PTE

Supporting local industry.

LEFT: 116, the second of the two Tiger Cub chassis with Pennine bodywork of similar layout to the Marshall bodies on Nos 111-114, the first four.

CENTRE FAR LEFT: 'Can't tell the back from the front' features. The rear window was of the same dimensions as the front windscreen on the Pennine bodied Tiger Cubs as shown by 115 posed here when new at Alexandra Park in 1965. *(J. J. Holmes collection*

BELOW: Perhaps spartan, even slight clinical, interior. *(All: Ribble Enthusiasts' Club)*

ABOVE: Now seen in action, the Matador prepares to rescue Leyland PD3/5 No108 on 3 November 1968 after its unfortunate collision with a tanker at the junction of Rochdale Road (near right) and West Street (near left and far right) in which 46 passengers were injured. The bus was on service 9, Ashton - Rochdale, during the evening peak period and although only 3½ years old, was scrapped. The upper saloon emergency exit has obviously been used to good effect. Temporary kerbstones were already in place and the AEC Matador breakdown tender is preparing to recover 108. *(Oldham*

The Atlanteans were not only of distinctive appearance but incorporated some special features. 121-171 were of type PDR1/1 Mark II, those up to 160 powered the 9.8-litre O.600 engine uprated by 5bhp to 130bhp and those with higher numbers by the 150bhp 11.1-litre O.680 unit. There was no side-view "bustle" effect caused by the rear engine compartment as side shrouds were incorporated. The influence of Liverpool's bodywork specification was evident. The roof domes were peaked, the lower saloon floor level raised, and the back-to-back seats over the rear wheel arches included. Passenger movement was helped by the flat floor between the staircase and the nearside front wheelarch on which there was extra luggage space. The windscreens and upper saloon front windows were in V-

BELOW: Numerically the first of Oldham's Atlanteans, a PDR1/1 Mark II with Roe bodywork, 121 is posed at Alexandra Park when newly delivered in 1965. The styling of the 77-seat body was an example of the move originating within the operating industry to break away from the bland and even ugly appearance of some bodybuilders' products on first-generation rear-engined double-deck chassis from the late 1950s (Roe included, it has to be said, although in mitigation the design was from Park Royal). In Oldham's case the light upperworks helped, and the V-shaped front windows and a lowered upper saloon waistrail also detracted from an originally uninspiring outline. The specification of the interior appointment was high and a further commendable feature was the clarity and legibility of the lettering on the blinds *(Oldham Evening Chronicle)*

formation, a fashion to gain popularity for many years, although upper saloon side windows were a little shallower than those downstairs. As with all Roe bodywork on rear-engined chassis, Park Royal steel frames were used. Two translucent roof panels were featured and much use again was made of plastics materials internally. The front destination layout, positioned high, was generally similar to that on the PD3s but a new entry on the route blind read "FOG ON ROUTE", to be shown at the driver's absolute discretion when a journey was to be ended short of its terminus (as with Manchester's shorter display, "FOG"). Most of the Atlanteans were several hundredweight heavier than the PD3s, the dual-doorway examples reaching nearly 9¼ tons.

It was intended originally that only the bodies of Atlanteans 125-130 should be built by Roe, the order for those of 121-124 going to East Lancashire Coachbuilders of Blackburn which was then controlled by the John Brown Engineering Group. Its products were a common sight elsewhere, especially in Lancashire, but it could not meet Oldham's delivery dates and so Roe built all ten bodies. East Lancashire had produced some attractive Atlantean bodies specified by Mr Ralph Bennett, General Manager of Bolton who later achieved wider fame in Manchester and London. Oldham's 131-135 had East Lancashire bodywork to the Bolton-inspired design incorporating equal-depth side windows to both saloons and a one-piece curved windscreen. When given the order for 148-152, the Blackburn builder transferred the work to its subsidiary Neepsend Coachworks of Sheffield for quicker delivery, using the design of 131-135.

From 1964, Oldham's double deckers were of greater length but the Passenger Transport Department was going to greater lengths to specify its requirements in the interest of passenger-amenity. Clearly, the placing in service of such up-to-date and stylish vehicles as the Atlanteans engendered much civic pride. Most regrettably, the events that took place later in 1965 were to cause embarrassment and humiliation. What happened was that an inspection carried out by Ministry of Transport vehicle examiners,

beginning on 11 October 1965, resulted in PSV7 'stop' notices being issued to 97 buses, 42 per cent of the 233-strong fleet. Many of the faults were with bodywork, some of a minor nature such as torn upholstery, but this did not detract from the sense of shock created. The immediate need was to maintain service levels and this was done by hiring buses from other municipalities. Five of the suspended vehicles were dealt with and returned to service the same day. Eight followed the next day, a further ten on the third day and another 24 within a week.

The following were deemed beyond economic repair and withdrawn forthwith:

249*/263/266	(Leyland PD1/3)
297	(Crossley SD42/3)
312*/316*/335	(Daimler CVD6)
366	(Crossley DD42/8)

Dismantled for spare parts before scrapping

The 45 hired buses comprised 32 Leylands (6 from Bolton, 2 Bury, 10 Manchester, 3 St Helens, 5 Sheffield, 2 Stockport, 4 Wigan), seven AECs (3 Bradford, 4 Rochdale) and six Daimlers (Salford), fuller details appearing in Appendix 1. Bradford's AECs were returned first due to the high cost of hiring. The Daimlers were Gardner-engined and like the AECs were non-standard in Oldham. Two of the Wigan buses had lowbridge bodies. The borrowed vehicles were intended for Monday - Friday peak time duties and so little was seen of them during daylight, minimising embarrassment. As some of them had the same fleet numbers as Oldham buses the odd mix-up did occur, such as when a driver starting with an all-day bus duty on limited-stop service 10, Greenfield - Manchester, carried out an instruction to "take 411" which was an Oldham Leyland. Unfortunately the first 411 he saw was a Salford Daimler.

Although it was unusual for an operator of Oldham's size and status to have so many buses suspended, it was not unheard of. Two years previously, Cardiff Corporation had

65

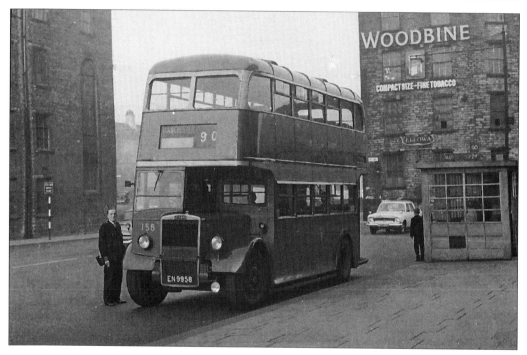

1965 crisis-1

UPPER: Blue and cream Bradford Corporation 209, one of three 70-seat Metro-Cammell-bodied AEC Regent Vs of 1964 borrowed to cover Oldham's vehicle emergency, stands at the Hollinwood end of service 8 to Shaw. *(J. J. Holmes)*

CENTRE: In light green and cream, Bury Corporation's 158 is a 1949 Leyland Titan PD2/3 with classic Weymann 58-seat bodywork, one of a pair on loan. It stands here in Rochdale before leaving on the fast service 90 for Manchester, a name conveniently already on Bury's blinds. *(J. J. Holmes)*

LOWER: One of ten Manchester buses involved was 3176 of 1949, a Leyland Titan PD1/3 with typically flamboyant Manchester styling to its 58-seat Metro-Cammell body in cheerless red. Two similar buses and seven all-Leyland PD2/3 Titans made up the Manchester contribution *(J. J. Holmes)*

1965 crisis—2

UPPER: Oh, what a classically elegant bus! Many enthusiasts would probably agree that the combination of AEC Regent Mark III chassis and Weymann bodywork of the period around 1950 as exemplified here by Rochdale's ivory and blue 229 was hardly surpassed for attractiveness. The afternoon sun provides floodlighting at Wallshaw Street and the destination display is that of Rochdale which did not do short workings of service 9 south of Thornham, called 'Summit' on Oldham blinds. *(J. J. Holmes)*

CENTRE:. This garage line-up shows the buses of thee contributing operators. Nearest the camera is E76, a member of the trio from St Helens in their attractive scarlet and cream, each a 1954 Leyland Titan PD2/10 with 56-seat Davies body on Park Royal frames. Second and fourth are two of the half-dozen from Bolton, 427/438 respectively, all-Leyland Titan PD2/4 models (a variant peculiar to Bolton) in Bolton's sober but smart brownish maroon and cream livery. Third from the camera is one of the six Metro-Cammell bodied Daimler CVG6s from Salford (407-412) in that city's impressive dark green and cream.
(J. J. Holmes)

LOWER: Out of the gloom comes Salford Daimler 412 with distinctive and robust Metro-Cammell bodywork. An almost triangular rearmost offside lower saloon window and, just out of sight, a rectangular staircase window are evidence of the fitting of a Birmingham-style straight staircase which encroached more into both saloons and reduced the seating capacity to 54. The bus is about to go on service G to Alt, as shown by the board in the nearside front bulkhead window. Note also the long destination blind handles. Behind, Oldham Crossley-bodied Daimler 333 prepares to operate a short working of service D to Washbrook as crews finish or start their duties, or take their break. *(J. J. Holmes)*

1965 crisis—3

UPPER: Five tin front Titans were sent by Sheffield, 835 being shown here with a similar bus behind. All were 1957 PD2/20 chassis with Roe 58-seat bodywork carrying what was once described as Sheffield's "bravely impractical" livery of cream relieved by three blue bands. They were of similar outline to many Oldham buses of the 1950s and the pair dominate this animated scene at Shaw (Wren's Nest) with an Oldham Roe-bodied PD1/3, a Crossley-bodied Daimler and an all-Crossley DD42/8 filling in.
(J. J. Holmes)

CENTRE: Stockport's fleet of the 1960s was often viewed as somewhat conservative and is exemplified here by 25, a red and cream East Lancashire-bodied Leyland Titan PD2/40 and one of two on loan. Although only one year old, its specification included 27ft length, forward engine, part-synchromesh gearbox, winding quarter-drop windows and exposed radiator, the only concession to post-1954 thinking being a seating capacity of 64. However, it was a sound and reliable combination and, disregarding crew labour costs, relatively inexpensive to operate compared with some other types then in service. An Oldham destination blind has been fitted although the original sevice number blind is retained.
(J. J. Holmes)

LOWER: Two of the four Wigan buses hired were lowbridge, needed to negotiate the many bridges with slightly less than 14ft 6in headroom in the Wigan area. 25, finished in maroon with ample white relief and very traditional numerals and lettering, was a 1949 all-Leyland PD1 with 53 seats, those in the upper saloon arranged in benches of four (the rearmost one was for three) with low roof and sunken offside gangway to keep the overall height to about 13ft 6in. Alongside the destination indicator were the green lights which distinguished Wigan Corporation buses from those of other operators on their home ground during darkness. Behind, Sheffield 834 climbs West Street and a Manchester Corporation Metro-Cammell bodied PD2 (not on hire to Oldham) has just come up from the big city on part-day limited-stop service 34 (later 134).
(J. J. Holmes)

had 46 buses treated similarly. A report by Oldham Passenger Transport Committee's Maintenance Sub-Committee was presented to the Council on 2 February 1966. Its principal points and recommendations were:

1 Discussions had been held with union personnel; foremen; consultants; management; MoT Area Mechanical Engineer.

2 Oldham's spending on maintenance had been relatively low. Despite increasing costs, during 1958-61, spending had gone down by 15 per cent, lowering morale and affecting labour relations.

3 50% of the fleet was more than 15 years old. There had been a shortage of labour for maintenance, aggravating the situation.

4 Oldham had tended to buy its buses in relatively large batches with insufficient provision in capital estimates for replacement out of revenue. Decisions to remedy this in 1942 and 1954 had not been implemented. The fleet replacement reserve had not been implemented until 1959/60 and then only at £15,000 a year. This was about the cost of only two buses in 1965.

5 An advantage of planned fleet replacement programme (FRP) was that it avoided peaks and troughs of maintenance.

6 During the first two years of the FRP, 26 new buses had been purchased out of capital at a cost of £166,756 [see note *A, below]. As at Feb 1966 a further 17 were on order [note *B] at about £120,000, most of this to be met from revenue. Before the implementation of the FRP, only £187,500 of fleet replacement expenditure had been financed from revenue. Another 17 new buses were expected during 1966/67, totalling 60 under the FRP, or 25 per cent of the fleet [note *C].

7 Interim purchase of 12 second-hand buses to be made, to run for 2-3 years, of types for which spares were in stock [note *D].

8 Post-war fares had been too low; provision for renewing machinery and improving facilities had been inadequate.

9 Weaknesses had now been identified. A productivity bonus was being introduced. There would be some reorganisation. Expenditure, and consequently fares, would need to rise.

Notes on points in report

*A The 26 buses purchased (point 6) were Leyland Titan PD3/5s 101-110, Tiger Cubs 111-116 and Atlanteans 121-130.

*B The first quantity of 17 (point 6) comprised Atlanteans 131-147.

*C The second quantity of 17 (point 6) comprised Atlanteans 148-160 and Panther Cubs 117-120.

*D The 12 second-hand buses, 463-474, were purchased during winter 1965/66. A further four, 475-478, followed later in 1966.

SIXTEEN SECOND-HAND BUSES PURCHASED 1965 and 1966
All were Leyland-bodied Leyland PD2s from municipalities. Other details were as follows:

Oldham Fleet No	Reg No	From	Former Fleet No	New	Chassis type	Body code
463	LWE 104	Sheffield	604	1949	PD2/1	H33/26R
464-466	LWE 109-111	Sheffield	609-611	1949	PD2/1	H30/26R
467-470*	ACP 392/385/388/390	Halifax	308/101/104/106	1947/48	PD2/1	H33/26R
471-474	DBN 329/330/337/342	Bolton	426/427/434/438	1949	PD2/4	H32/26R
475-478	OWB 856/857/859/861	Sheffield	656/657/659/661	1952	PD2/10	H33/28R

*Prepared and repainted in Oldham livery by Halifax. Others by Neepsend Coachworks, Sheffield

PD2/1—26' x 7'6", vacuum brakes.   PD2/4—26' x 8', air brakes.   PD2/10—27' x 7'6", vacuum brakes

BELOW: Purchased in the aftermath of the 1965 crisis were four Leyland Titans from each of Sheffield, Halifax and Bolton, followed by four more from Sheffield, all sixteen having Leyland bodies. Now as Oldham 471 with fleet number plates, this ex-Bolton PD2/4 is about to overtake stationary PD2/1 No 470 with transferred fleet numerals, ex-Halifax. Note the similarity of destination and service number indicators with a subtle difference. The location again is the spacious and well-lit Wren's Nest terminus at Shaw, 471 being on service 3 to Mills Hill and 470 on service 8 to Hollinwood. *(J. J. Holmes)*

RIGHT: 476, an all-Leyland PD2/10, was one of four bought from Sheffield in 1965, following four PD2/1s from that source. It is seen emerging from the shadows into Egerton Street while on a diversion. *(J. J. Holmes)*

CENTRE RIGHT: Shrouded, but not in mystery, Roe-bodied Atlantean 138 reveals the partial covering-in of the rear bustle as was standard on Oldham Atlanteans except for the final twelve, which were delivered to the PTE. The livery seen here is pommard and cream. *(J. J. Holmes)*

The arrival of the second-hand buses enabled most of the remaining Crossleys and Daimlers to be withdrawn, along with some Leyland PD1s and PD1/3s. Those acquired from Halifax lasted until 1968 but the others exceeded predictions and survived to enter the SELNEC fleet in 1969.

As to new vehicles, there were some detail differences between batches of Atlanteans including, from 131, hinged engine side covers. East Lancashire-bodied 131-135 entered service in February/March 1966 and eleven of the 136-147 Roe dozen arrived in August. 146 was delayed until October as it was a Commercial Motor Show exhibit for Roe and differed in several respects. It had a full-length translucent roof panel instead of two short ones and, to be standard on Oldham's future Roe Atlanteans, a Smith's 1500-type automatic heating system. Neepsend-bodied 148-152 and Roe 153-160

entered service during April/March 1967 respectively, 159 uniquely having hopper window vents instead of top-sliders.

A change to regulations in 1961 had allowed the maximum two-axle bus length and width to become 36ft and 8ft $2^{1}/_{2}$in (increases of 6ft and $2^{1}/_{2}$in). Oldham's next new

RIGHT: While Roe bodied most of the Leyland Atlanteans placed in service from 1965, there were also five from East Lancashire Coachbuilders and five of virtually identical appearance from its subsidiary, Neepsend Coachworks (148-152). In the recently introduced pommard and cream livery, 152 here parades along Glodwick Road. Note the absence of dark band at cantrail-level and the large one-piece curved windscreen which is not matched by the upper saloon front windows. (Copyright holder not known)

LEFT: Negotiating the notorious Jubilee bend on the bridge over the Rochdale - Oldham railway loop line between Shaw and New Hey, new 1966 Roe Atlantean 145 has just left New Hey for Manchester on limited stop service 2. *(J. J. Holmes)*

CENTRE LEFT: When new in 1967, Roe-bodied Atlantean 159 was unusual in having hopper-type window vents which were soon replaced with the normal sliding variety. This was the bus encountered by the author near Perth in 1994, still at work conveying farm labourers. *(Copyright holder not known)*

ABOVE: 159 is captured here in Mumps after receiving top-sliding window vents. *(J. Fozard)*

LEFT: Seven of the 1966 Roe-bodied Atlanteans, 153-159, are posed here before entry into service. Double headlamps were an Oldham feature for several years. *(GMTS)*

edged in the Atlantean type-designation until an 'A' suffix was added for the gearbox later. 165-168/171 entered service in the new year. Following collision repairs in 1969, 168 came out with front indicators positioned just above the windscreens and were operable from downstairs. 1965 Atlantean 126 subsequently received the same treatment. As an encouragement for operators to renew their fleets, Government grants of 25 and subsequently 50 per cent were to become available for new buses from 1 September 1968, subject to certain conditions which included suitability for driver-only operation. The first five buses to which this applied were on order and to become 178-182. To augment them, 161-171 were adapted to be worked by driver only. 168 was also fitted with a cab periscope.

On 1 April 1968, all services with identifying letters were numbered as set out in Appendix 1. Although no further new double deckers arrived in 1968, when Crossley 368 was withdrawn the fleet became all-Leyland for the first time since 1925. There had been ten saloons in the fleet since 1950 but with the arrival in April 1968 of Marshall-bodied Panthers 172-177 the total became sixteen. The new

buses were the 45-seat Marshall-bodied Leyland Panther Cub PSRC1/1 saloons, 117-120, entering service in April/ May 1967 and built to an intermediate length of 33ft 6in. Produced only during 1964-68 when just 94 examples were built, the Panther Cub was a shorter version of the more powerful full-length Panther. Both had an underfloor engine mounted horizontally behind the rear axle and in the case of the Panther Cub this was the 6.54-litre O.400 as in the Tiger Cub. It had to work exceptionally hard in Oldham as the unladen weight of the Panther Cubs was practically 7¾ tons. These new Leylands ousted the remaining Crossley saloons.

Although from 1 July 1966 driver-only operation had been legalised on double deck buses, Oldham restricted it to single deckers initially, introducing it on 29 August 1966 on the Royton - Shore Edge service, redesignated from F to 17. With the introduction of the Panther Cubs, driver-only operation was extended to the other single deck services and the vehicles were equipped accordingly. The services were C (later 15), Higgin-shaw - Middleton Junction (Mainway); and 16 (E until 1966), Oldham - Mossley (Brookbottom).

Atlanteans 161-171 began to arrive from Roe in December 1967. They introduced the O.680 engine and instead of the previous Atlantean electro-pneumatic type of gear control, had the fully-pneumatic form as fitted to the Tiger Cubs and PD3/5s. Both of these features were to be standard but neither was acknowl-

be demolished. On 15 January 1969 it was decided to introduce a bus service for Sholver as soon as conditions on the estate permitted. Existing services along Ripponden Road from Chadderton Hall Park were 5 to Strinesdale and 6 to Denshaw. While service 5 remained unchanged, some journeys on 6, and additional ones, were routed via Sholver (in and out the same way) as service 4 (now a disused number), some terminating at Sholver.

The Transport Act, 1968, was now on the Statute Book and preparation was being made for the formation of the Passenger Transport Authority and its operating Executive, embracing Oldham and ten other operators in the Manchester area, to come into existence on 1 November 1969. Oldham's final buses to be delivered and first new ones built for driver-only operation were Atlanteans 178-182 of type PDR1/1A. They entered service in April 1969, others on order not arriving before the PTE era. Much thought had gone into the detail design. Features included a wider cab, gear-change on the right (leaving the driver's left free for fare collection), spring-operated parking brake, forward-ascending staircase near the centre exit, cab periscope, passenger-counter, electrically-heated windscreen, two opening translucent roof panels and an additional reversing light in the skirt panel ahead of the nearside rear wheel arch, illuminating the kerb. In service, the driver-only Atlanteans displayed a stylised coin-slot symbol either side of the front destination indicator. The new buses began running on services 25/26, Town

buses were type PSUR1/1, 36ft long and with the optional O.680 engine, fully-pneumatic gear control and 17ft 6in wheelbase, one foot shorter than standard and allowing a longer front overhang with wide entrance. Seating and standing capacity were 48 and 20 respectively and although equipped for driver-only operation when placed in service they were restricted to crew-operated route 22—previously D—Rhodes Bank–Moston (Greengate), due to their front overhang. Along with the 153/155 Uppermill Circular service, this became driver-only operated on 29 December 1968.

At that time, a new housing estate was being built near Moorside off Ripponden Road at Sholver, an ancient district named in the Domesday Book as Sholgher. Wild and exposed, on a west-facing slope at an altitude of nearly 1,000 feet, it was perhaps a dubious spot for such a development and within 20 years many of the dwellings were to

ABOVE: No 179, second member of the pioneering batch of five 1969 Atlanteans built for driver-only operation from new, shows itself at work with the 'coin-in-slot' symbols on either side of the destination screen, these denoting the ticketless fare-box system. *(R. Marshall)*

Hall - Holts, converted to driver-only operation on 8 June 1969. A maximum of nine buses was needed and four of the adapted 161-171 batch were added to 178-182 to meet requirements.

Although the end was now in sight for Oldham as a transport undertaking, all traces of it would not disappear overnight. Indeed, many buses of Oldham origin were to remain in service throughout the relatively short existence of SELNEC and pass to the succeeding Greater Manchester PTE in 1974, some of them lasting well into the 1980s.

RIGHT: The coat of arms of the former County Borough of Oldham as applied to the Corporation's buses. The motto translates from Latin as *'dare to be wise'*. *(J. J. Holmes)*

The idea of an area transport board based on Manchester was first discussed in 1931, as has been mentioned. It was to crop up again times over the years and the sequence of events is outlined below.

1931 On 9 July, Oldham Tramways Committee discussed the possible formation of a joint municipal transport board for Ashton-under-Lyne, Manchester, Oldham, Rochdale, Salford, Stockport "and other adjacent districts." Initial approaches to Manchester Tramways Committee and the Cheshire Tramway Authorities Council came to nothing but the idea was not to be forgotten.

1935/36 The concept was revived during 1935 in the wake of the setting up of the London Passenger Transport Board on 1 July 1933. Serious discussions followed but on 9 September 1936, Oldham Passenger Transport Committee was told that all municipalities in the area except Oldham, Manchester and Salford had withdrawn. Oldham then pulled out.

1937 A further meeting was convened in Manchester on 19 January, attended by representatives of the railway companies and municipal and private bus operators, including Oldham. It was decided to set up a committee to investigate the co-ordination of all passenger transport in what later was called Greater Manchester. Membership comprised one representative each from the Ashton-u-Lyne, Bolton, Bury, Manchester, Oldham, Rochdale, Salford, SHMD Joint Board and Stockport undertakings; the LMS and LNE Railways; and the Lancashire United, North Western and Ribble bus companies. Oldham's representative was the PT Committee Chairman, Alderman Isaac Crabtree. He attended the first meeting on 15 March but there was little enthusiasm and no progress was made for many years.

1947 The Labour Government's Transport Act of that year aimed at nationalising all forms of transport. It envisaged the setting-up of area schemes, the first of which was to be in north-east England where it was considered that the predominance of Labour councils would minimise opposition. This was not to be the case. Generally they were reluctant to let go their transport undertakings and

BELOW: Ordered by Oldham but delivered in PTE colours in 1971, 5188 was the first of a dozen Leyland Atlanteans that would have been Oldham's 188. It is seen newly delivered in the garage. *(J. Fozard)*

the same message was sent out by the newly-constituted South-East Lancashire and East Cheshire Joint Advisory Committee, of which Oldham was a member. If there was to be a change, it was in favour of combining municipal bus and tram operations only. None of the proposals got off the ground and after a change of Government in 1951 they were dropped.

1963 On 19 June, a meeting was held in Manchester of local authority representatives from south-east Lancashire, north-east Cheshire and north-west Derbyshire, to discuss a proposed survey of a possible future organisation of transport. Oldham took part but again there were no positive results.

1966 By this time many operators were having financial difficulties due to falling traffic and rising costs. In July, a Labour Government White Paper entitled *Transport Policy* was published. It envisaged the setting-up of four

conurbation transport authorities, one of them based on Manchester (the others being Merseyside, Tyneside and West Midlands). There were also provisions for the funding of public transport (including railways) by councils, with Government capital grants for the purchase of new buses to approved specifications and suitable of driver-only operation. The proposed organisations were to consist of: *(a)* the Authority (PTA), a political body comprising representatives of the councils in the area; and *(b)* the Executive (PTE), a body of professional people responsible for operations. These proposals were enshrined in the Transport Act, 1968.

1967 Meetings were held of the Steering Committee with representatives from the 11 municipal operators and three companies in the area (Ashton-u-Lyne, Bolton, Bury, Leigh, Manchester, Oldham, Ramsbottom, Rochdale, Salford, SHMD, Stockport; Lancashire United, North Western, Ribble). It dealt with preliminary matters such as the standardisation of concessionary fares and charges for dogs and luggage. The Manchester area undertaking was to be named the South-East Lancashire and North-East Cheshire PTA, in practice abbreviated to the acronym SELNEC, and formed on 1 April 1969. The PTE would take over the 11 municipal undertakings on 1 November 1969. Oldham was represented on the PTA initially by Cllr E Leeks, the PT Committee Chairman.

1969 At midnight on 31 October, the Oldham municipal transport undertaking ceased to exist. It became a constituent of SELNEC Southern Division which included the former

Ashton, SHMD and Stockport undertakings. Mr Harry Taylor became Chief Engineer of SELNEC Central Division. Apart from the legal lettering on the vehicles, nothing changed immediately.

As related previously, outstanding orders comprising Roe-bodied Atlanteans 183-187/188-199 were delivered to SELNEC in 1970/71 respectively, the former five in Oldham colours despite the fact that in December 1969, Atlantean 171 (later 5171) had been the first ex-Oldham bus to appear in SELNEC sunglow orange and off-white. Repainting into the new livery was a somewhat lengthy process. Even after its introduction, some older buses were repainted in pommard and cream, with SELNEC markings, and these colours were still around as late as 1975, after the disappearance of SELNEC. A bizarre episode was the transfer to Oldham depot early in 1970 of ex-Stockport all-Leyland PD2/1, 302, which was repainted into *pommard and cream* and given the SELNEC number 5202 in error, later corrected to 5922!

On 1 April 1970, the PTE commenced its own vehicle numbering system. Buses were re-numbered generally in blocks that bore some relation to their previous numbers. Gradually, ex-Oldham buses were withdrawn, some of the earlier ones before their new numbers had been applied. In 1970, the exposed-radiator PD2s and the sole surviving PD1/3 went, and inroads were being made into the tin-front PD2s. Only one PD2 and two sin-

gle deckers are believed to have survived 1975. The remaining PD3s were withdrawn in 1977, the earliest Atlanteans in 1978 and the final buses that had operated for Oldham Corporation, 179/180/182, in 1982. 180 had been newly repainted by mistake in Greater Manchester PTE's revised orange, bitter chocolate and white livery! The last Oldham-specified bus, 5194, was withdrawn in 1984. Some former Oldham buses saw various forms of service elsewhere and as late as the mid-1990s, the author was astonished while driving along the Perth—Dundee road to encounter ex-Oldham Atlantean 159, still in orange and off-white, hurrying in the opposite direction while in use with a Tayside farmer for workers' transport. Particulars of renumbering and withdrawals are contained in Appendix 3.

BELOW: When in 1981 the Greater Manchester PTE revised its livery format to orange with white about the upper saloon waistrail and bitter chocolate skirt panelling, it was applied erroneously to Atlantean 5180 (originally Oldham 180) not many weeks before its withdrawal. The result is seen here as it turns into Mumps. *(Author)*

Early Post-War Busman

"Oh, they were swines!" That was Arnold Blomley's description of the pre-war Crossley buses (or 'Crozzley buzzes' around Oldham!). Returning unscathed from the Far East during the war, Arnold had started working "on t' buses" of Oldham Corporation as a conductor. Three months later he passed for driving and did that job during 1946-54. "Say you were on split shift and going out on an afternoon workmen's at about half past four. What you did, when you came in after the first part of your shift, was to look on the board to see what bus you'd have later on. If you'd got a pre-war Crossley, before you did anything else you went down the rows to find it and you started the damn thing up. If you didn't, when you came to take it out you couldn't change gear till you got to Shaw! That was because on cold days the oil in the 'box was so thick it slowed down the moving parts and made it difficult to move the lever. Running the engine in the garage kept it a bit warm. Heavens, those Crossleys were shocking. And the travel on the gear lever to get it into third: well, if you were small you had a heck of a job with it. This is perfectly true: it sounds funny, but there were one small bloke driving on Shaw. They used to swear there were no bloomin' driver on t' bus because he'd gone right under t' dashboard to get it into third gear! If you didn't get it in you'd look up quick to see where you were then go back under again for another try. It were like going down the mine! The steering and everything could be heavy as well. Doing a workmen's with a Crossley was like doing a whole shift. You were tired when you got back.

"We used to get the Daimlers on workmen's, too. The drivers weren't keen on them in spite of their preselectors. I'll tell you why. It always seemed to happen to me in one place: going up Greaves Street from Union Street. You'd just get about twenty yards up, near t' back o' t' Town Hall, and you had to change down. If you didn't press the gear-change pedal right down it would spring out beyond its normal position. You could get a nasty knock on the left leg from it. What you'd to do then was to push the pedal back in, putting your hands on the cab ceiling to push yourself down, using all the strength in your left leg. They were a menace. But I always used to appreciate the outline of those Roe-bodied Leyland TD5s with CBU registrations. D'you know, I think they were the bonniest bus ever made. With all those nice curves and the radiator, and that beautiful livery with the lining-out, well, in my opinion they haven't bettered it since. I honestly did enjoy driving those pre-war Leylands. Shall I tell you what I really liked best about them? The push-on handbrake. It was the best handbrake of any vehicle I've ever driven. You just pushed it on like that, and to release it you just pushed it a bit further until it clicked off the notch and it came back steady. You could let it off as easy as anything in the palm of your hand.

"When I learned bus-driving the Chief Instructor was

Inspector Hulme. He would advise using the clutch-stop for a quicker gear-change. You'd to give the pedal a full stab and make a quick movement of the gear stick, but let the pedal up slowly. Many a time you'd miss it at first and it'd make a hell of a racket. But we had good instructors. Hulme used to say, 'You don't drive a bus from the front. You drive it from 100 yards ahead. Anticipation: that's what good driving's about. And if you work with your mirrors all the time, you'll be a good bus driver. I want to be able to sit on your bus with a glass of water full to the brim and you should be able to go from Oldham to Manchester, stopping at all the stops, without a drop being spilt.' And," added Arnold, "I've tried to keep to that in all my driving ever since.

"When I first started driving my guard [conductor] was Ronnie Webb. What a character! He'd started as a tramway points lad at Star Inn. Well, he was always buzzin' off and leaving 'em queued up! He'd have more trams stood in a line than goodness knows what. One of my driver-mates had a nasty shock one day. He was driving one of the first Leyland PD2s going to Moorside. It'd only been in service for a few days. When he stopped at the iron railings he felt a shudder and wondered what'd caused it. Then he saw a wheel bowling itself across the road. It landed on t' Town Hall steps. 'Whose wheel's that?' It was his own! Luckily nobody was in the way or else they might have been killed. But of course the police had to become involved. And it was a brand new bus! Yes, we had a hard job keeping time, with being busy all day and then it was harder as the road traffic increased. The inspectors used to say, 'We won't book you for running late, even if it's half an hour, but if you're a minute early, we will.' My most regular route was the O/T from Hollinwood to Lees and Grotton, busiest route in Oldham. You'd pick up a good load at Hollinwood and then all the way up Hollins Road there'd be more. You'd drop a lot but pick up another lot at Suburbs. Then you'd lose a lot at the top of Copsterhill Road but pick plenty up at Primrose Bank. Then you'd lose most of 'em at Market but pick up as many again. Oh, it was like that all the way. And if you'd a bad bus and a bad guard it became the banana route: the buses ran in bunches because they wouldn't pass you. They'd all be up each other's staircases.

"In any batch of buses you'd get variations between individual ones. One might be a bad puller, another would have heaving steering, another would have a difficult gearbox and so on. You'd be taking over on the road and see it coming. Then you'd think, 'Good 'eavens, do I have to put up with this thing all bloomin' night, or shall I change it over?' Word used to go round, what they were like. Well, in 1954 I fancied a change so I left the Corporation and went driving wagons."

Arnold Blomley, characterful, popular with those who knew him, passed away in 1991.

Wartime Clippie - for 38 Years

"I left my job in a cotton mill and started conducting in 1941," recounted Mrs Edith Powell, one of those who responded to the appeal for female conductors during World War 2. Some fifty years later she too was enjoying a well-earned retirement in her native village of Lees. "We had to have a medical and the doctor had misgivings about me because I was so thin! My height was 5ft 6in but I weighed only 7½ stone. Still, they took me on. We were told it was a temporary job and they'd finish us when the men came back from the war. But I stayed for 38 years! Of those who started at the same time, I was the last to leave when I retired from the PTE in 1979.

"Oh, there were more than 200 of us wartime clippies. Our training covered a fortnight and was all unpaid. We had four days indoors and the rest out on the road with established conductors. It was so complicated for a newcomer, what with all the joint working arrangements. There seemed such a lot to remember. Anyway, I persevered and got my licence and badge, number CC 31164. It was always hard work. Early in the morning or late at night I had to walk to and from Lees, about a mile and a half each way. I knew every step in the blackout. And we were always so very busy! In the peak there were 33 buses leaving the garage almost together for Shaw. We had to get people to and from work. There was one journey that went to Shaw from the garage at about 4.30 in the morning. We'd pick up a full standing load at the first stop! I don't know where they all came from but most of them must have had to walk some distance to the bus.

"We were on the go all the time. There was never a moment to rest our weary limbs. Even if there had been, we wouldn't have dared! One inspector, if he saw you sitting down, would report you and write 'Idle Jack' on your waybill. And we had to book-up at every stage. Yet I always managed to do it. You had to get into the habit of doing everything quickly. The main problem in the blackout of course was that we could hardly see, the lighting inside the buses was so dim. They gave us small battery lamps but they were unreliable and not much use. It was hard to see where you were punching tickets and you had to be careful about foreign coins. During the war, we also had those gas buses. Oh, they were terrible! The smell from the furnace on the trailer was dreadful. We were supposed to stoke them up. Well, we didn't know how to do it, did we? Nobody liked them. The buses would hardly go. We were all glad when they got rid of them.

"The first General Manager I worked for was Mr Richards. Oh, he was a gentleman. He always travelled by bus and would sit upstairs at the front, leaving us free to do our job. He didn't want us to think he was watching us. After about three years, Mr Paige came and after him for about the last seven years before the PTE it was Mr Taylor.

"When I started, after things had settled down my regular routes were the 5/6/H group, Chadderton - Denshaw. The passengers up at Grains Bar and Denshaw were always so kind to us. In those days of rationing they would sometimes give us packets of tea and fruit and stuff. Of course we did work all over the system but mostly on the same routes. Latterly, when driver-only operation came in, the number of conductor services dwindled and in PTE days I ended up on 427/429 which had been O/T, Hollinwood - Lees or Grotton.

"My own regular driver at first was Frank Higgins. A couple of years later it was Eddie Cross and we crewed together for nearly 37 years. One day in 1946, I was working with a new driver who had just come off the trams. I don't know how he did it but instead of going down Yorkshire Street he managed to swerve to the left of the iron railings and the bus didn't stop until the front wheels were on the steps of the war memorial! Luckily, no-one was injured but it gave me a fright. The weather could be cruel, too. In the snows of early 1963 the bus before us had managed to get out of Denshaw but we got stuck in a drift and had to 'phone for assistance. It was two hours before they got through with the wagon and some chains. I was never so cold in all my life! Another time, a few years later I think, there were severe floods at Denshaw. The water was well up the sides of the bus. We used to have really thick fog, too, but it never stopped us. One day it was so thick that my driver couldn't see the edge of the road. We were on route 8 and I actually had to walk all the way from Hollinwood, up through Werneth and along through Royton to Shaw, on the kerb at the front of the bus to guide him. Fine weather could mean more work for us. Say you were spare crew on a nice Sunday afternoon. If the crowds began to build up for Greenfield or Denshaw you would have to do extra journeys to take them, and then go back for them later.

"I never like working on the Crossleys. Somehow I just didn't feel safe on them. One day we had a Crossley, coming out of Denshaw. Just as we got up to Grains Bar there was an almighty bang and the engine began to make a loud knocking noise. What a racket! We kept going down the hill and I was looking across to the right all the time because at the other side of that little stone wall there was a big drop. The driver told me it was a big end gone. I wasn't so keen on the Daimlers, either, and most of the drivers used to say they were hopeless. I remember once talking to a well-to-do passenger at Denshaw about them. I think he was a retired military officer but I said, 'The posh folk ride about in their expensive Daimler cars but we have to put up with this kind of Daimler rubbish!' He laughed at that.

Well, when I was getting near my retirement they wanted me to stay on for a while, but I decided not to. I'd enjoyed being on the buses for all those years, in spite of the hard work and unsocial hours. In 38 years I was never late once and never off sick. There was always comradeship and we had plenty of laughs. I never had much trouble with drunks because I found that if you were tactful and tried to be nice they wouldn't bother you. I was never in a collision in which anyone was hurt. It wasn't a bad experience for a temporary job!"

Clearly, Mrs Powell had found satisfaction in doing a demanding and difficult kind of job. She had become well known and respected among regular passengers for her courtesy and efficiency. It was a pleasure to meet her and hear her reminiscences.

The Michelin Man

James Fletcher was a tyre fitter at Oldham Corporation bus garage from 1954 to 1979, when he retired. He was employed by the tyre manufacturer and not the Corporation, which was usual, and in Jimmy's case it was Michelin. This company had the tyre contract for all even-numbered buses in the fleet. The odd-numbered ones had Dunlop tyres, although there were a few exceptions to this rule.

"We checked the tyres every day," Jim recalled. "This was done by tapping them with a hammer. If the sound was hollow it meant the pressure was too low. We could tell pretty accurately. The Corporation kept records of tyre mileage. When a tyre had run all its miles it had to be replaced. A worn tyre could be re-cut. We'd keep on re-cutting a tyre until we came to the canvas. Yes, it was all quite safe and legal.

"When I started, there was a fleet of 240. That meant I was responsible for 120. It was a lot of tyres. In fact, if you reckon it up, it was 720. I started working for Michelin through a relative. He told me about this vacancy. 'Tyre fitter?' I said. 'I can't fit tyres!' 'Just come with me,' he replied. 'You'll be all right.' So I went and got started. I'd had no previous experience but Michelin just showed me what to do and I got on with it. I had doubts at first because I'm just over five foot tall and I've never had the weight. But I managed the job OK. Some of the garage lads would have a bit of a laugh at times. They'd say they'd seen this flamin' great wheel coming down the garage all on its own. Then they'd realise I was behind it!

"All the tyres were cross-ply with inner tubes originally. Then later on there came tubeless and radial-ply. They gave higher mileage. We'd to make sure we never mixed cross and radial on the same axle, and that the front tyres on a bus were fairly evenly worn. It didn't matter about the rear. When a bus was over the pit we'd go down and have a good look at the inner rears for cuts and other damage. The job could be dangerous, too. One day a bus had a puncture at Hollinwood. Well, tyre fitters weren't supposed to go out but for some reason there was no-one else and they asked me to go with them to change the wheel. I was just jacking it up and I'd stood the spare wheel against the wall. Some young lads were larking about and the wheel fell over and landed on my foot. I was off work thirteen weeks with a broken ankle. Then another time we all had a shock when my mate on Dunlops was killed when his wheel brace bar broke while he was working on a bus. Aye, there could be a lot of hazards in tyre-fitting.

"I went into the tyre store one day when there was a stranger in. It was a bit suspicious and so I said, 'What d'you want? You're not supposed to be in here. Go on, get out!' He went, and never said anything. Later on I found out it was Harry Taylor, the new Deputy General manager. Of course when I saw him next, I apologised. When Oldham had at big to-do with a lot of buses being put off the road in 1965 it was mainly on account of mechanical and bodywork faults. There was nothing wrong with the tyres.

"I never saw a great deal of the Michelin people. The area manager would come in about every six weeks. I had to keep my own records and send them to the Michelin office in Burnley every week. If I needed anything special I had to 'phone them. They used to send me their monthly bulletin. This gave me all the news about developments in tyres and equipment.

"No, I didn't think I'd be able to do the job at first. To start with, I found it hard. But like everything else, there was a knack to it. You had to take all the strain with your legs, not your back, and use your weight to best advantage when you were levering. When you had to put a wheel on the back platform of a bus, you didn't need to lift it. You just stood it against the platform edge and let it fall over then shove it into position. You always had to make absolutely sure the jack was safe. Bear in mind, it wouldn't be the first time a jacked-up bus had dropped down. At the rear, we'd jack up under the axle, below the spring. You weren't supposed to go under a bus with a wheel off if it was supported only by the jack.

"I had to laugh one day. They started a new lad and I asked him to take a wheel off. Next time I looked he was having a problem. 'What are you doing?' I asked. 'I'm loosening the wheel nuts,' he replied. 'No you're not, you're tightening them,' I told him. He didn't realise the nearside nuts had left-hand threads. Yes, I've had some hard times but there've been some laughs and I enjoyed the job although it was tiring. The bus garage was a good place to work but when I reached retirement age in 1979 I was glad to sit back and take a rest."

Jimmy Fletcher was still enjoying his retirement in the 1990s. All those to whom his name has been mentioned have spoken of his amenable nature and willingness to oblige.

Oldham Leylands in Colour

UPPER LEFT: Leyland Atlantean 170, one of eleven received in 1967/68, is seen from a vantage point above the hairpin bend at the Cross Keys, Delph, amid typical Pennine surroundings. *(J.J.Holmes)*

CENTRE: 445, from the batch with aluminium-framed upper-deck, climbs West Street and passes the original four-level part of the Civic Centre. *(Photobus—Arnold Richardson)*

LOWER LEFT: Part way on its fast run from Greenfield to Manchester, 409 passes through Oldham with the Town Hall in shade on the right and *th'iron railins* on the left of the picture. *(Photobus—P. Eckersley)*

UPPER LEFT: Crimson lake liveried 418 basks at Stevenson Square, Manchester terminus of the Waterhead 98 service. *(Photobus—Roy Marshall)*

CENTRE: Older Oldhamers will remember Gartside's Ales, carried by the Bedford lorry alongside bus 437 in pommard livery at the Star Inn. *(G. W. Morant)*

LOWER LEFT: For heaven's sake wash those mucky marks off the tin front! 453, with Northern Counties body is seven minutes out of Waterhead and is due to reach its Manchester destination in another 39. *(G. W. Morant)*

UPPER RIGHT: The striking appearance of the exposed radiator Leyland Titan PD3s is somewhat marred in this view by the dirty state of bus 106, seen here at Mumps Bridge. *(G. W. Morant)*

CENTRE RIGHT: Blue hues for 402 but it just wasn't Oldham! It is caught in Union Street on its way down from Greenacres to Limeside. *(Photobus— Roy Marshall)*

LOWER RIGHT: Manchester's Stevenson Square is the setting in which Atlantean 133 is pictured before another journey up to waterhead on the 98. *(G. W. Morant)*

Some examples of tickets described in Chapter J

Geographical (left) and numerical tickets from Bell Punch days

(All tickets in upper and centre rows from the collection of Glyn Weigh)

Pre-printed returns from 6½d to 1/1d printed by Williamsons.

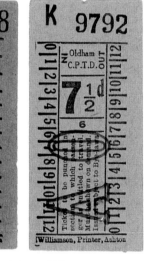

A 4½d child's return

An Oldham–Rochdale, a Joint and an Ashton–Oldham

A 4d 'workpeople's return'.

(All tickets in bottom row from the collection of S. H. Hughes)

A ½d and a 1d numerical stage single — reverse shown opposite.

A "geographical" 2d workpeople's daily return for Hathershaw–Summit route available up to 8am for return the same day

A "numerical stage" 8d workpeople's daily return with large red R overprint.

A throuh ticket for the Ashton–Rochdale service blue AOR overprint

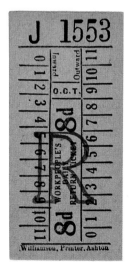

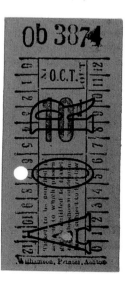

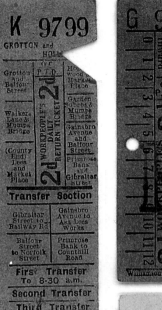

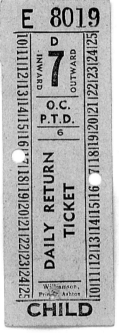

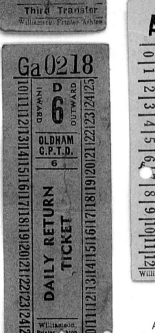
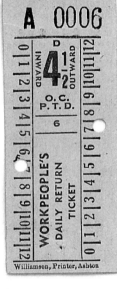

A characterful array of tickets showing the variations in size and type of ticket.

Top left shows advertising seen on the the reverse of many tickets. Oldham people still remember the general grocer shops with pale blue tiled fronts, known as Brown's Stores, of which there were several branches in the town.

Of particular interest is FC2094 (bottom row) a rare one for the Mossley service, the return part cancelled in an idiosyncratic manner using thumb and forefinger.

Also of interest is the last example (C4474) with the unusual face value of 1/0½d (one shilling and a ha'penny).

(All tickets on this page from the collection of S. H. Hughes)

85

Ticketing Systems

In tramway days and on Oldham buses until the 1950s, conductors issued pre-printed tickets, the batches of each value kept firm in a spring clip on a hand-held wooden rack. Holes were punched in the tickets to validate them by means of a bell punch worn on a strap. Tickets were obtained for many years from the well-known printers and suppliers, Alfred Williamson of Ashton-under-Lyne. After mechanisation other suppliers such as Oller and the Bell Punch Co, both of London, were also used.

Until the late 1920s, Oldham's tickets were of the common "geographical" type with the names of the fare stages printed in box sections down each side. In early years, holes were punched in the stage boarded and that to which the ticket was valid. Subsequently only the latter was done. Later still, "full geographical" tickets were introduced. These contained in each section the names of both stages between which the passenger could travel for the fare paid, the hole being punched as appropriate. The punch registered the total number of holes it made. Moreover, every tiny paper disc created by the holes remained inside the punch. As each value of ticket was a different colour, these minute fragments could be counted, labour-intensively, to check the number of tickets of each value issued, and the total, against the number on the register dials.

Between the stage names, tickets had a centre section containing references to the regulations and the initials "OCT", "OCPTD" or later, "Oldham CPTD", or perhaps a description of the ticket. At the top of each one an identification mark appeared, comprising a letter or letters and number. Two examples would be: 1d single Fn 7593; Workpeople's Daily Return Ticket J 1539. Below the number was the name of the service such as "Hathershaw & Summit".

From the late 1920s, Oldham began to adopt "numerical stage" tickets although workpeople's "geographical" examples survived at least until 1949. The "numerical" ones had the fare stages on each route numbered 0-11, later 0-12, and printed down each side with those on the left side for inward journeys and those on the right for outward. Obviously there was more room for numbers than for names and the tickets could be issued on any service. This saved printing costs. The hole was punched in the number of the stage to which travel was available except in the case of some returns, when the system was reversed. Mechanised ticket-issuing was first considered in 1934 but nothing happened for ten years. The newly-appointed Mr Paige then reported to the Committee on the subject but again, no action was taken.

A notable World War 2 item was the "re-board" ticket. When evacuating a bus or tram at the sounding of the air raid alert, passengers were given one of these tickets from a roll, entitling them to board the vehicle again after the sounding of the all-clear.

Joint services

Although fairly conventional for many years, Oldham's tickets were both varied and idiosyncratic due to the diversity of joint bus and tram operations. A joint service required agreements between operators on such matters as:

- how each would contribute to the total scheduled mileage through the number of vehicles allocated and the order in which they would run;
- whether through fares would be offered or passengers would be required to re-book at the boundary between operating areas;
- how expenses and receipts would be apportioned;
- whether one operator would issue the other's tickets in the other's area.

Manchester - Waterhead

From the introduction in 1907 of the joint Manchester - Oldham Corporations through tram service, the "area booking" system was used and this continued on the succeeding 98 joint bus service during 1946-51. Through passengers in each direction re-booked at Hollinwood. In the Oldham area (Waterhead - Hollinwood), whether on an Oldham or a Manchester vehicle, they received Oldham tickets under Oldham regulations, and vice-versa on the Hollinwood - Manchester section. Each undertaking supplied the other with the necessary tickets. However, the respective ticket value colours of each operator were not all the same, as shown in this list:

Value	Manchester	Oldham*
½d	lilac	brown
1d	white	white
1½d	green	yellow
2d	cerise	blue
2½d	yellow	salmon
3d	salmon	cerise
3½d**	purple	purple
4d**	orange	orange (originally grey)
5d**	bright green	bright green (originally lilac)

Oldham tickets supplied to Manchester Corporation for the Waterhead route were in Manchester's colours, not Oldham's.

**Apparently not used in tramway days.*

Ashton - Oldham - Rochdale

These services, operated jointly by all three undertakings, also had ticketing complexities. The first through-running facility was limited-stop bus service 7, introduced in 1928 with its own range of tickets having "AO&R Joint Service" title. As with other limited-stop services, "area booking" did not apply. Single fares were relatively high but cheap returns were available in these colours:

Adult:

9d buff; 10d white; 1s 0d orange;

1s 6d pale buff; 1s 9d green.

Child (overprinted "CHILD" in red):

5d blue; 6d primrose; 11d grey

9d child—9d adult issued instead;

All three operators used the same return tickets and while originally they also used "AO&R Joint Service" singles, apparently they began soon to use their own singles, especially in the commoner lower values. Some of the more obscure value tickets up to 11½d for this service were never used up and Oldham Corporation was issuing them on other services as late as 1950! Of the original joint single tickets, these colours are known to have been used:

3d	red
5d	green
5½d	brown
8½d	violet with red stripe
9½d	apple green with red stripe
10½d	brown with red stripe
11½d	pink with red stripe

When limited-stop service 7 was replaced by normal service 9 on 19 February 1939, there were changes. On any bus, local passengers received tickets as follows:

Ashton - Hathershaw, Ashton tickets;

Hathershaw - Summit, Oldham tickets;

Summit - Rochdale, Rochdale tickets.

There were some exceptions comprising minimum-fare overlaps across boundaries and some special joint through tickets. Otherwise, cross-boundary fares were simply the total of the relevant local single fares and passengers were issued with two or even three tickets when they booked. While there were no ordinary returns, local workpeople's returns survived. There were five new joint through tickets, applying to the commonest journeys, and overprinted with large capital outlines as shown below and supplied by Oldham Corporation to Ashton and Rochdale:

Ashton - Oldham	AO*	4½d
Rochdale - Oldham	RO**	6d
Ashton - Royton	AO*	6d
Ashton - Rochdale	AOR**	10d
Rochdale - Royton	RO**	5d
Outlines:	*red	**blue

From about 1948, as with other joint tickets on the system, these tickets were given the prefix numbers 3 or 4 to their index letters according to the operator to whom supplied, for example, 3Nk 0279 to Ashton, 4Jf 2870 to Rochdale. The original service 9 through fares were unchanged until 31 March 1951 when there was a halfpenny rise on those to and from Ashton. This was followed by a further similar rise on all through fares a year later when the "AOR" overprint was replaced by the word "JOINT" in red or blue, enabling the tickets to be used elsewhere also.

Manchester joint limited-stop services

The fares on these were stable and uncomplicated with through ticketing and returns. However, service 90 from Rochdale had a 1s 3d workpeople's return and also a weekly ticket, both available up to the 8.30am departure from each end compared with Oldham's 8 o'clock time limit. Oldham had its own workpeople's returns for this service, increased to 1s 6d then 1s 8d before mechanisation on the limited-stop services in 1956. Those returns did not need fare stage numbers as there was only that one example available on service 90 and the words "Rochdale and M'chester" appeared at the foot of the centre section. Down each side were printed the days Monday - Saturday, those on the left for inward journey cancellation and those on the right for outward.

Joint service 59, Manchester - Shaw

This long and sinuous route via Cheetham Hill, Middleton and Oldham, run jointly by Oldham and Manchester, had special Oldham tickets overprinted with "JOINT" for short bookings across the area boundary at Mills Hill, that is, Thurland Street (Chadderton) - Hilton Fold Lane (Middleton). Cross-boundary passengers otherwise received one ticket of each operator appropriate to either side of Mills Hill. These should have been issued together but it seems that some Manchester conductors at busy times issued only one and then went through the bus again at the boundary in order to re-book through passengers.

Other joint services

From Oldham these were: E, to Mossley, joint with SHMD which numbered it 16; N, to Stalybridge, joint with SHMD and Ashton which numbered it 8; and P, Uppermill Circular, joint with North Western which numbered it 153. All were free from complex area booking although the Mossley service had joint return tickets.

The 'Ultimate'

After some experiments, it was decided in 1950 to hire 150 "Ultimate" ticket machines from their supplier, the Bell Punch Co. The original annual charge was £5 per machine, reduced to £4 10s 0d if allocated to one specific conductor. These machines, which were not used on limited-stop services, had five barrels for pre-printed tickets of different values although future examples had six. By 1954, Oldham had 262 Ultimates on hire. They were speedy machines to operate when only one ticket was being issued but due to the high number of fares on some services it was frequently necessary to issue two or more tickets in combination. While this slowed the process it was still quicker than with the rack and punch system. An Ultimate ticket was only 3cm long and 2.7cm wide, much less than half the size of a punched ticket. Gradually, tickets were altered so that all joint operators' colours were the same. The Ultimate was introduced on service 9 by all three operators in 1954, each using its own tickets. "Area booking" was abolished and passengers were booked through with one ticket, or one strip of tickets. For some months after the change, though, Oldham still used punched tickets on some peak time journeys, issuing its own local tickets throughout.

Setright introduced

Ticketing on the limited-stop services was updated in 1956 when machines supplied by Setright Registers Ltd of Bow, London, were introduced. The Setright was a robust box-shaped machine that printed its own tickets measuring 6 x 2.5cm, of any value up to 19s 11½d, from one blank roll. It had two concentric fare-selection dials on the top, the outer one for pence and the inner for shillings. Further concentric dials below those for fares set the month, the day and the stage number, and a small knobbed lever selected the class of ticket. The tickets were numbered 000-999 in sequence.

A TIM experiment

In 1964, following further tests, twelve TIM machines were purchased from their manufacturer, Ticket Issuing Machines Ltd of Cirencester, at a total cost of £696. Tickets measured 8 x 3.8cm and as with the Setright, their values were "dialled". In addition to the usual details, the machine printed

ABOVE LEFT: A five-barrel example of the Bell Punch Co "Ultimate" machine is worn by the conductor of this Roe bodied Leyland PD2/20 at Holts. *(GMTS)*

ABOVE RIGHT: "Just like that!" Conductor Bert Harrop demonstrates how to issue a ticket from a TIM (Ticket Issuing Machines Ltd) instrument. *(Oldham Evening Chronicle)*

LEFT: Driver Tommy Monks turns away from the steering wheel to issue a ticket from an "Ultimate" ticket machine, fitted experimentally. The "passenger" is Ms Rene Trigg of the garage clerical staff. *(Oldham Evening Chronicle)*

the service number and year. Regrettably, subsequent records on the acquisition of TIM equipment are vague but machine numbers are known to have reached 27 at least. A quantity of used ones from Bolton brought the total to about forty. Original Oldham examples stamped the tickets with "OCPTD" and those from Bolton simply had that town's name obliterated, leaving the word "Transport".

When the first driver-only services began in 1966, five new electrically-driven TIMs were used. Six similar ones were obtained the following year for service expansion. In 1969, however, when the first double deck driver-only service commenced, the Johnson Fare Box system was employed, no tickets being issued and no change given. Due to abuse, however, it was not to last for long.

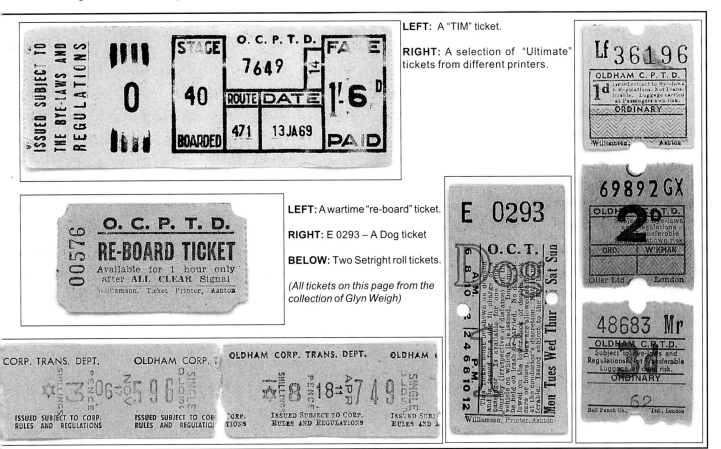

LEFT: A "TIM" ticket.

RIGHT: A selection of "Ultimate" tickets from different printers.

LEFT: A wartime "re-board" ticket.

RIGHT: E 0293 – A Dog ticket

BELOW: Two Setright roll tickets.

(All tickets on this page from the collection of Glyn Weigh)

X DEPOTS

Bus garages

1913-19   Copsterhill Road

Former tram depot which was also used for garaging and storage of the two trolleybuses, 1925-30. It was adapted for use by motor buses but was not convenient to the routes. The site was still in use by Oldham Metropolitan Borough Council in 1996.

1924-26   Dogford Road, Royton

Former Bury, Rochdale & Oldham Tramways Co Ltd (previously Manchester, Bury, Rochdale & Oldham Steam Tramways Co) steam tram depot with dual gauge lines and separate entrances for each gauge—3ft 6in and 4ft 8½in. The premises were subsequently adapted for use as a bus garage but it was not situated conveniently for bus routes. Dogford Road has been industrial premises for some years and remains in existence in 1996.

1926-38   Henshaw Street

One of the highest bus garages in the country at an altitude of 750ft, it was extended in 1929 but, again, it was not conveniently near bus routes—although better than Dogford Road—and was unsuitable for further extension to accommodate the growing bus fleet in the 1930s. The site was disposed of and the building was subsequently demolished and virtually no trace of it has remained for many years.

1938-69   Wallshaw Street

These are purpose-built premises, comprising offices and garage, off Mumps, on many bus routes and with spacious and modern facilities. Wallshaw Street passed to SELNEC, and GMPTE. It remains in use in 1996 with FirstBus, to which group Greater Manchester Buses now belongs.

Bus Services Operated

Items of particular note are mentioned in the text. Other major developments are included in the tabulations below and in the periodic lists of services.

Note. In the notes below, the following symbols and abbreviations are used to denote joint operators with Oldham CPTD and other details where appropriate:

*a	Ashton-u-Lyne Corporation	*r	Rochdale Corporation
*h	Halifax Corporation	*s	Stalybridge, Hyde, Mossley & Dukinfield Joint Transport Board
*m	Manchester Corporation	dd	double deck operation, otherwise single deck
*n	North Western Road Car Co	♦	limited-stop service

Early Development

Date commenced or revised	Description and revisions	Notes
12 May 13	Werneth Hall Rd - Coppice St - Wellington Rd - Coppice (Windsor Rd) *See text*	dd
10 Aug 15	Altered to: GPO–Coppice (Chamber Rd/Windsor Rd) via Napier St E instead of Werneth Hall Rd	
13 Sep 19	*Withdrawn*	
14 May 13	Moorside - Grains Bar *Replaced by tramway extension*	dd
4 Jun 14		
31 Aug 14	Grains Bar - Denshaw	dd
27 Aug 16	*Withdrawn*	
	No bus services operated from 14 September 1919 to 14 December 1924	
		Route letter/ number and/ or notes
15 Dec 24	Hollinwood Stn - Manchester Rd - Chamber Rd - Coppice St - Napier St E - Union St W - Union St - Mumps Stn	A from 28 Feb 25
16 Mar 25	Altered to: Chapel Rd - then Chamber Rd - then as above to Union St - then Greenacres Rd - Greenacres (Cemetery)	
6 Apr 27	Extended: Greenacres - Heywood St - Waterhead - Scouthead	dd from 1926
8 Mar 28	Cut back from Scouthead to Greenacres (Yew Cres)	
14 Oct 29	Greenacres terminus altered to Cemetery *See service A in subsequent lists*	
28 Feb 25	Chadderton Rd (Tram Terminus) - Burnley La - Broadway - New Moston (Broadway/Moston La)	B
25 Jul 25	Altered to: Royton Stn - Broadway - New Moston (Manchester Boundary)	
29 Aug 25	Altered to: Royton Stn - Broadway - Failsworth	
30 Jul 27	Altered to: New Hey - Royton Stn - Broadway - Failsworth - Woodhouses	
19 May 30	Merged with Shaw - Manchester and Chadderton - Manchester services to form new service: New Hey - Shaw - Royton - Broadway - Chadderton - Newton Heath - Manchester (Lr Mosley St) *See service 2 in subsequent lists*	2, *m *n ♦
1 Aug 25	Clegg St - Union St - King St - Middleton Rd - Lansdowne Rd - Fields New Rd - Thompson La - Foxdenton La - Eaves La - Middleton Junction	C
29 Sep 26	Oldham terminus altered to Star Inn *See service C in subsequent lists*	
20 Aug 25	Rhodes Bank - Union St - Crossbank St - Manchester St - Oxford St - Block La/Butler Green	D
28 Jan 27	Extended: Block La/Butler Green - west end of Coalshaw Green Rd	
6 Jan 35	Extended: Coalshaw Green Rd - Long La *See service D in subsequent lists*	
23 Jan 26	Oldham (Town Hall) - Lees Rd - Springhead - Coverhill Rd - Mossley (Brookbottom) *See service E in subsequent lists*	E
2 Apr 26	Hathershaw - Ashton Rd - King St - Rochdale Rd - Royton - Summit	7, dd
1 May 28	*Replaced by tram service*	
1 Jan 27	Town Hall - Waterloo St - Abbeyhills Rd - Manor Rd *See service G in subsequent lists*	G, dd
6 Apr 27	Shaw - H Crompton - Dogford Rd - Royton - Streetbridge - Mills Hill *See service F in subsequent lists*	F

Date	Description	Code
15 Apr 27 28 Jul 27 27 Aug 30	Oldham - Grains Bar - Denshaw - Rishworth - Ripponden - Sowerby Bridge - Halifax Altered to: Oldham - Grains Bar - Denshaw Merged with Market Pl - Moorside (6) & Grains Bar (5) services *See services 5/6/H in subsequent lists*	H, *h *n
12 Aug 27 15 May 29 25 Oct 31 4 Dec 32	Oldham - Lees - Springhead - Grotton - Grasscroft - Greenfield Extended: Oldham - Manchester Rd - Hollinwood - Newton Heath - Manchester (Lr Mosley St) Manchester terminus altered to Parker St Altered to run via Hollins Rd instead of Manchester Rd *See service 10 in subsequent lists*	J *m *n ♦
22 Feb 28	Ashton - Hathershaw - Oldham - Royton - Summit - Rochdale *See services 7 (this route)/9/M in subsequent lists*	7
8 Mar 28 15 May 29 19 May 30	Shaw - Royton - Featherstall Rd - Hollinwood - Newton Heath - Manchester - Didsbury - Gatley Cut back from Gatley to Manchester (Lr Mosley St) Merged with Chadderton - Manchester and New Hey - Woodhouses services to form new service as shown previously for service 2 *See service 2 above and in subsequent lists*	*m *n ♦ 2, from Mar 1930
8 Mar 28 15 May 29 25 Oct 31 4 Dec 32	Scouthead - Oldham - Manchester Rd - Hollinwood - Newton Hth - Manchester - Didsbury - Gatley Extended Scouthead - Uppermill, running from Oldham alternately via Scouthead (13) & Lees (14) Cut back from Gatley to Manchester (Parker St) Altered to run via Hollins Rd instead of Manchester Rd *See services 13/14 in subsequent lists*	*m *n ♦ 13/14, from Mar 30
2 May 28 20 Oct 30	Market Pl - Lees - Springhead - Grotton, *replacing trams to Lees* Some journeys cut back from Grotton to Lees (County End) *See services O/S/T in subsequent lists*	O, dd
24 Sep 28 15 May 29	Summit - Royton - Chadderton - Newton Heath - Manchester (Lr Mosley St) *Withdrawn*	*n ♦
24 Dec 28 27 Aug 30	Market Pl - Ripponden Rd - Moorside (6) or Grains Bar (5), *replacing trams* Merged with Denshaw service (H) as: Market Pl to Moorside (6) or Grains Bar (5) or Denshaw (H) *See service H above and services 5/6/H in subsequent lists*	5/6, dd 5/6/H
15 May 29	Uppermill Circular (Oldham GPO - Scouthead - Delph - Dobcross - Uppermill - Greenfield Stn - Grasscroft - Grotton - Springhead - Lees - Oldham GPO) *See services P/153/155 in subsequent lists*	P, *n
9 Dec 29 19 May 30	Chadderton (Burnley La/Garforth St - *note, some sources state Town Hall*) - Newton Heath - Manchester (Mayes St) *(former Tognarelli service)* Merged with Shaw - Manchester and New Hey - Woodhouses services to form new service as shown previously for service 2. *See service 2 above and in subsequent lists*	*n 2 *m *n ♦
19 May 30 29 Nov 30	Middleton - Chadderton - Failsworth - Woodhouses *Operation taken over by North Western Road Car Co*	159
16 Jun 30 8 Nov 31	Oldham - Manchester Rd - Hollinwood - Newton Heath - Manchester - Palatine Rd - Northenden Cut back from Northenden to Manchester (Parker St)	34 *m ♦
30 Apr 32 6 Jan 35 12 Jun 35	Derker (Sydenham St) - Market Pl - Chadderton Rd - Chadderton (Burnley La/Broadway) Extended: Chadderton (Burnley La/Broadway - Burnley La/Clogger Hill) Altered to: Derker (Sydenham St) - Market Pl - Coldhurst - Booth Hill Chadderton section linked with Moorside (6) and Grains Bar (5) section, *replacing Market Pl - Chadderton Rd trams* *See services B below, and 5/6 in subsequent lists*	B dd from 6 Jan 35 5/6, dd
24 Apr 34 12 Jun 35	Star Inn - Booth Hill Merged with Derker - Booth Hill *See service B/12 in subsequent lists*	B, dd
12 Jun 35 12 Jun 35	Shaw (Wren's Nest) - Higginshaw - Market Pl - Middleton Rd - Mills Hill Shaw (Wren's Nest) - Higginshaw - Market Place - Mills Hill - Middleton - Rhodes - Heaton Park - Cheetham Hill - Manchester (Cannon St), *both bus services replacing trams on Shaw - Market Pl and Market Pl - Middleton sections* *See services 3/59 in subsequent lists*	3, dd 59, dd *m

Note: The events outlined in the tables above were the significant moves in the establishing of Oldham's bus service network. Subsequent developments were generally the replacing of tram services and the altering of existing bus services either to rationalise them or to serve new housing areas. The lists to follow reveal the trends that were to emerge over the years to 1969.

Tramway replacement programme, 1935-46

Note: Tram services replaced before 1935 are mentioned in the tabulations above

Date withdrawn	Date commenced	Service	Description
11 Jun 35	-	tram 3	Market Pl - Middleton Rd - Mills Hill - Middleton
11 Jun 35	-	tram 9	Shaw (Wren's Nest) - Higginshaw - Market Pl - Chadderton Rd
-	12 Jun 35	bus 5/6	Grains Bar (5) - Moorside (6) - Market Pl, both extended to Chadderton (Burnley La/Clogger Hill)
-	12 Jun 35	bus 3/59 (59 *m)	Shaw (Wren's Nest) - Higginshaw - Market Place - Middleton Rd - Mills Hill (3) - Middleton - Rhodes - Heaton Park - Cheetham Hill - Manchester (Cannon St) (59) *m
21 Dec 35	-	tram 12	Market Pl - Hollins - Hollinwood
-	22 Dec 35	bus O	Grotton or Lees (County End) - Market Pl - extended to Hollins - Hollinwood
6 Nov 37	-	tram 4	Circular (Town Hall - Glodwick Rd - Park Rd - Town Hall)
-	7 Nov 37	bus 4/V	As tram service 4 - bus 4 clockwise (Glodwick Rd - Park Rd), V anti-clockwise (Park Rd - Glodwick Rd)
6 Nov 37	-	tram 7	Hathershaw - Ashton Rd - King St - Rochdale Rd - Royton - Summit
-	7 Nov 37	bus M	As tram service 7
	7 Nov 37	bus 9	As tram service 7, continuing to Rochdale *r *Note.* Additional part-replacement of tram service 7 was provided by limited-stop bus service 7, Ashton–Oldham–Rochdale, joint with *a *r, commenced 22 Feb 28 . Bus service 7 was withdrawn on 18 Feb 39 and replaced the following day by service 9, extended south from Hathershaw to Ashton and forming a new Ashton - Rochdale service, joint with *a *r, with normal stops. Hathershaw - Summit short workings continued in operation by OCPTD as service M
2 Dec 39	-	tram 8	Shaw (Wren's Nest) - Royton - Featherstall Rd - Manchester Rd - Hollinwood
-	3 Dec 39	bus 8	As tram service 8
3 Aug 46	-	tram 20 *m	Waterhead - Market Pl - Manchester Rd - Hollinwood - Newton Heath - Manchester (Stevenson Sq)
-	4 Aug 46	bus 98 *m	As tram service 20. Tram and bus joint with *m
	4 Aug 46	bus 1	Short workings, Waterhead - Hollinwood

List of bus services—31 March 1935—in order of introduction

Letter/ number	Description	Notes
A	Chapel Rd - Greenacres	dd
C	Star Inn - Middleton Junc	
D	Rhodes Bank - Long Lane	dd
E	Oldham (Town Hall) - Mossley (Brookbottom)	*s
G	Town Hall - Manor Rd	dd
F	Shaw - Royton - Middleton	
34	Oldham (Market Place) - Manchester (Parker St)	dd *m *n ♦
10	Greenfield - Oldham - Manchester (Parker St)	*m *n ♦
7	Ashton - Oldham - Rochdale	*a *r
13/14	Uppermill - Scouthead (13) or Lees (14) - Oldham - Manchester	*m *n ♦
O	Market Pl - Grotton	dd
2	New Hey - Manchester	*n ♦
H/5/6	Market Pl - Moorside (6) - Grains Bar (5) - Denshaw (H)	dd
P	Uppermill Circular	*n
B	Derker - Chadderton (Burnley La/Clogger Hill)	dd
	Booth Hill - Star Inn	

List of bus services—30 July 1944

Note. In this and subsequent lists, services are in alphanumerical order and double deck-operated except where sd (single deck) shown

Letter/number	Route	Notes
A	Chapel Rd - Greenacres	
B	Derker - Booth Hill	
C	Star Inn - Middleton Junc	sd
D	Rhodes Bank - Moston (Greengate)	
E	Oldham (Town Hall) - Mossley (Brookbottom)	sd *s
F	Shaw - Royton - Middleton	sd
G	Town Hall - Abbeyhills	
H	Market Pl - Denshaw	
M/9	Ashton (9) - Hathershaw (M) - Oldham - Summit (M) - Rochdale (9)	9 *a *r
N	Oldham (Town Hall) - Hurst - Stalybridge *(commenced 10 Apr 36)*	*a *s
O/T	Hollinwood - Hollins - Lees (County End) (O) or Grotton (T) (see S, below)	
P/153	Uppermill Circular (clockwise P, anticlockwise 153) *(OCPT on 153 at peaks only)*	*n
S	Heron St - Clarksfield Rd (short working of O/T)	
V/4	Circular (clockwise V, anticlockwise 4)	
2	New Hey - Manchester (Parker St)	*m *n ♦
3/59	Shaw (Wren's Nest) - Higginshaw - Oldham - Mills Hill (3) - Manchester (Cannon St) (59)	59 *m
5/6	Chadderton (Burnley La) (6) - Westhulme Av (5) - Moorside (6) - Grains Bar (5)	
7	Chadderton (Victoria St) - Higginshaw (short working of 3/59)	
8	Shaw (Wren's Nest) - Royton - Hollinwood	
10	Greenfield - Oldham - Manchester (Parker St)	*m *n ♦
13/14	Uppermill - Scouthead (13) or Lees (14) - Oldham - Manchester (Parker St)	*m *n ♦
24	Rochdale - Chadderton - Manchester (Parker St) *(service acquired from Yelloway Motor Services, Feb 44)*	*m *r ♦
56	Hollinwood Av - Manchester (Victoria Av E/Rochdale Rd) *(operated by MCT only but jointly-licensed)*	sd *m

List of bus services — 27 August 1956

Letter/number	Route	Notes
A	Chapel Rd - Greenacres	
B	Fitton Hill - Middleton Junc Stn	
C	Strinesdale - Middleton Junc	sd
D	Rhodes Bank - Moston (Greengate)	
E	Oldham (Town Hall) - Mossley (Brookbottom)	sd *s
F	Shore Edge - Royton (Town Hall)	sd
G/7	Higginshaw (Boundary) - Limeside (Acacia Rd or Laburnum Rd) (7 - both directions), or Holts - Limeside (Laburnum Rd) (7 - one direction only) Limeside (Laburnum Rd) - Holts (G - one direction only) or Town Hall - Holts (G - both directions)	
H	Market Pl - Denshaw	
M/9	Ashton (9) - Hathershaw (M) - Oldham - Summit (M) - Rochdale (9)	9 *a *r
N	Oldham (Town Hall) - Hurst - Stalybridge	*a *s
O/T	Hollinwood - Hollins - Lees (County End or Stamford Rd)(O) or Grotton (T) (see S, below)	
P/153	Uppermill Circular (clockwise P, anticlockwise 153)	*n
S	Heron St - Clarksfield Rd (short working of O/T)	
V/4	Circular (clockwise V, anticlockwise 4)	
1/98	Waterhead - Werneth - Hollinwood (1) - Manchester (Stevenson Sq) (98)	98 *m
2	New Hey - Manchester (Stevenson Sq)	*m *n ♦
3/59	Rushcroft (3) - Shaw (Wren's Nest) (59) - Higginshaw - Oldham - Mills Hill (3) - Manchester (Cannon St) (59)	59 *m
5/6	Chadderton (Burnley La) (6) - Westhulme Av (5) - Moorside (6) - Grains Bar (5)	
8	Shaw (Wren's Nest) - Royton - Hollinwood	
10	Greenfield - Oldham - Manchester (Lever St^)	*m *n ♦
11/12	Derker - Stottfield (11) - Middleton (12)	
13/14	Uppermill - Scouthead (13) or Lees (14) - Oldham - Manchester (Lever St^)	*m *n ♦
24	Rochdale - Chadderton - Manchester (Stevenson Sq)	*m *r ♦
34	Oldham (Market Pl) - Manchester (Stevenson Sq) *(part-day; operated by MCT but jointly-licensed)*	*m ♦
56	Hollinwood Stn - Manchester (Victoria Av E/Rochdale Rd) *(operated by MCT but jointly-licensed)*	sd *m
90	Rochdale - Royton - Manchester (Stevenson Sq) *(part-day; non-stop Royton - Manchester)*	*m *r ♦

^*Note. Lever St was adjacent to Stevenson Sq and Oldham Corporation bus destination blinds were set to show* Manchester, Stevenson Sq *on journeys terminating at Lever St*

List of bus services — 3 December 1966

Letter/ number	Route	Notes
A/H/7	Limeside - Chapel Rd (A) or Heron St (H) - Greenacres Limeside - Werneth - Bar Gap Rd (7)	
B	Fitton Hill - Middleton Junc Stn	
C	Higginshaw - Middleton Junc (Mainway)	sd
D	Rhodes Bank - Moston (Greengate)	
G	Town Hall - Alt or (one journey daily) Holts *(part-day)*	
M/9	Ashton (9) - Hathershaw (M) - Oldham - Summit (M) - Rochdale (9)	9 *a *r
N	Oldham (George Street) – Hurst – Stalybridge	*a *s
O/T	Hollinwood - Hollins - Lees (County End or Stamford Rd) (O) or Grotton (T)	
V/4	Holts - Abbeyhills - *Park Rd - Town Hall - Glodwick Rd* - Holts (4) (italicised section circular route) (converse - V)	
1/82/98	Waterhead - Werneth - Hollinwood (1) - Manchester (Stevenson Sq) (98) - Chorlton (82, operated by MCT)	98 *m
2	New Hey - Manchester (Stevenson Sq)	*m *n ◆
3/59	Rushcroft (3) - Shaw (Wren's Nest) (59) - Higginshaw - Oldham - Mills Hill - Middleton (3) - Manchester (Chorlton St) (59)	59 *m
5/6	Chadderton Hall Park - Strinesdale (5) or Denshaw (6)	
8	Shaw (Wren's Nest) - Royton - Hollinwood	
10	Greenfield - Oldham - Manchester (Lever St)	*m *n ◆
11/12	Derker - Stottfield (11) - Middleton (12)	
13/14	Uppermill - Scouthead (13) or Lees (14) - Oldham - Manchester (Lever St)	*m *n ◆
16	Oldham (George St) - Mossley (Brookbottom) (previously service E)	sd *s
17	Shore Edge - Royton (Town Hall) (previously service F)	sd
24	Rochdale - Chadderton - Manchester (Stevenson Sq)	*m *n ◆
34	Oldham (Market Pl) - Manchester (Stevenson Sq) *(part day; operated by MCT but jointly-licensed)*	*m ◆
56	Hollinwood - Cheetham Hill *(operated by MCT but jointly-licensed)*	sd *m
90	Rochdale - Royton - Manchester *(Stevenson Sq) (part-day; non-stop Royton - Manchester)*	*m *r ◆
153/155	Uppermill Circular (clockwise 155, previously service P; anticlockwise 153)	*n

Important notes

Joint operations: Not all joint operators would necessarily run on a jointly-operated service during the same period, or operate the same number of vehicles on a service permanently. Joint services were run on a basis of agreed mileage- and/or revenue-apportionment and at times it may have been necessary to balance the figures in accordance with agreements. This could be done by adjusting the number of buses, and therefore the mileage, run by each operator.

Journeys to & from bus garage: Generally, these were denoted by the letter X on the service blind of Oldham Corporation buses.

Football and rugby league special journeys: Journeys to and from Boundary Park (Oldham Athletic AFC) and Watersheddings (Oldham RLFC) generally displayed the service letter or number appropriate to their point of origin.

Re-designation of services — 1 April 68

The remaining familiar route letters were replaced by numbers on 1 April 1968. Some service numbers were altered at the same time. Moves toward the abolition of letters had begun in 1966, when the Oldham - Mossley service E had been numbered 16 (the number used by SHMD, the joint operator) and the Shore Edge - Royton service F had become 17. Details of the 1968 changes are outlined below.

Previous letter or number	Number from 1 Apr 68	Service
A	18	Limeside - Chapel Rd - Greenacres
B	21	Fitton Hill - Middleton Junc Stn
C	15	Higginshaw - Middleton Junc (Mainway)
D	22	Rhodes Bank - Moston (Greengate)
G	23	Town Hall - Alt
H	19	Limeside - Heron St - Greenacres
M	34	Hathershaw - Summit
N	8	Oldham - Stalybridge
O	28/29	Hollinwood - Lees (County End 28; Stamford Rd 29)
T	27	Hollinwood - Grotton
V	26	Holts - Town Hall (Circular)
4	25	converse of 26
8	20	Shaw - Hollinwood
34	134	Oldham (Market Pl) - Manchester (Stevenson Sq)

Appendix 2
Operating Terrain

Reference has been made to the hills on which Oldham is built. It is now time to travel over some of those hills on sample journeys in Corporation days. The first imaginary demonstration is on limited-stop service 13 from the humdrum streets of central Manchester to dramatic Pennine landscapes in Saddleworth, the view from Scouthead taking in Manchester, Cheshire, North Wales, Derbyshire and Yorkshire. Tables 1a/b give route details and an analysis.

Journey of contrasts

Table 1a
Service 13 : Manchester (Lever St) - Uppermill

Route locations	Time allowed (mins)	Miles from start	Altitude (feet)	Remarks
Manchester (Lever St)	-	-	150	Easy climbing to Failsworth along reasonably
Miles Platting	-	1.4	200	straight road through mixed
Newton Heath	-	2.3	250	industrial and old residential areas.
Failsworth boundary	-	3.1	289	Level stretches & gentle undulations to Hollinwood.
Hollinwood	18	4.8	354	Sharper climbing begins. 118ft rise in next mile.
Hollins Rd/Heron St	-	5.8	472	Densely-populated. Some industry.
Foot of Copsterhill Rd	-	6.1	542	More severe gradient - 91ft climb in 0.8m ahead.
Top of Copsterhill Rd	-	6.9	633	Slight descent then gentle climb before Star Inn.
Star Inn	-	7.2	643	Entering central shopping area.
Market Place	29	7.4	691	Busy interchange. Rise of some 540ft from start.
Mumps Bridge	31	8.0	594	Moderate descent from Market Place.
Huddersfield Rd/Ripponden Rd	-	8.6	679	Gradual climbing. Residential and industrial area.
Waterhead (near *Plough Inn*)	-	9.1	707	High hilly land in view but short descent ahead.
Waterhead (1/98 bus terminus)	-	9.4	650	Most arduous climb ahead. Less industry beyond.
Scouthead, *Three Crowns*	-	10.2	950	More sparsely-populated. Agricultural land around.
Doctor Lane Head	42	10.8	984	Exposed summit. Superb hill and dale panorama.
Near *Cross Keys*	-	11.7	784	Land rises sharply left, falls steeply right.
Delph (Station)	49	12.4	626	Snaking descent from Doctor Lane Head.
Dobcross, New Rd/Wool Rd	-	13.7	564	Gentle descent through scenic Upper Tame Valley.
Uppermill (The Square)	56	14.1	550	Picturesque Pennine village in sheltered dale.

Table 1b
Examples of height gained and lost over distance, Service 13

Locations	Height gained/lost (ft)	Distance (miles)	Ft/mile basis	Remarks
Manchester - Oldham (Mkt Pl)	+541	7.4	+73	
Manchester - Doctor Lane Head	+834	10.8	+77	Highest point of route
W'head (1/98 terminus) - Scouthead, *3 Crs*	+300	0.8	+375	Most arduous climb of route
Doctor Lane Head - Delph (Stn)	-358	1.6	-223	Longest/steepest descent

BELOW: The hilly terrain in and around Oldham is illustrated by this shot of Roe-bodied Leyland PD2/20, No 384, pulling into Abbeyhills Road in the mid-1960s. In the misty background is the tower of Hartshead Pike (940ft), between Oldham and Mossley, originally a Roman fire beacon and from which the counties of Lancashire, Cheshire, Derbyshire and the former West Riding of Yorkshire are in view (when clear!). *(J. J. Holmes)*

Test of skill

Service 10 from Manchester to Greenfield followed the same route as 13/14 to Mumps, and then 14 only to Greenfield Station. The No14 then continued ahead into Uppermill but 10 took a dramatic plunge at a hazardous spot. Tables 2a/b describe and analyse the route of service 10 from Mumps Bridge, quoting the mileage from the Manchester starting-point.

Table 2a
Service 10: Manchester (Lever St) - Greenfield (taking up at Mumps)

Note. *From Manchester. See Table 1a for details of route between Manchester and Mumps Bridge.

Route locations	*Time allowed (mins)	*Miles from start	Altitude (feet)	Remarks
Mumps Bridge	31	8.0	594	Short rise then level stretch then descent to come.
Lees Brook	-	9.3	544	Residential and industrial from Mumps.
Lees (County End)	37	9.8	600	Short climb from Lees Brook, then levelling.
Grotton (Hotel)	-	10.2	650	Arduous climb ahead. Agricultural land in view.
Lydgate (Crossroads)	-	10.8	856	Leafy residential area of large houses.
Greenfield Station (bridge)	47	12.1	650	Continuous descent from Lydgate. Now acute right turn from rail bridge down 0.2m hill at 1 in 8 with left hairpin bend half way down, then obtuse right turn on to canal bridge.
Canal bridge	-	12.3	525	Foot of rapid and hazardous descent into valley.
Greenfield (Clarence Hotel)	51	13.0	560	Scenic village surrounded by high hills.

Additional note

Double deck buses were not used on this service until 5 November 1941. Drivers were given special instructions to stop at the railway bridge when going to Greenfield and engage first gear for the descent of the hill. Leaving Greenfield they were instructed to stop at the foot of the hill and change to first gear for the ascent. Gear-changing on the hill was specifically prohibited. The sound effects from pre-war Leylands may well be imagined! In either direction the hill presented a challenge to proficiency and alertness.

Table 2b
Examples of height gained and lost over distance, service 10

Locations	Height gained or lost (ft)	Distance (miles)	Ft/mile basis	Remarks
Manchester - Lydgate (Crossroads)	+706	10.8	+65	Highest point
Grotton (Hotel) - Lydgate (Crossroads)	+206	0.6	+343	Most arduous climb of route.
Lydgate (Crossroads) - Canal bridge	–331	1.5	–221	
Greenfield Stn (bridge) - Canal bridge	–125	0.2	–625	Most hazardous descent.

BELOW : Marshall bodied Leyland Panther 176 is seen when new at the cross keys, Delph. The dramatic backdrop and skyline are typical of the region *(J. J. Holmes)*

ABOVE: At some 1,100ft the most elevated point on Oldham's transport system and highest former street tram terminus in Britain, Grains Bar is seen here in the foreground, looking south-west. Running left to right is Delph Road which forms a junction with the A672, at this point Halifax Road but called Ripponden Road beyond the bend on the extreme right. In the centre near background is Besom Hill, a promontory visible for many miles to the west. Sholver housing estate is to the right, and left of this is St Thomas's Church, Moorside. The valley of the River Beal is beyond, situated about 400ft below Grains Bar, and on its far side lie Heyside and Higginshaw. At the other side of Besom Hill, where the River Medlock rises, centre and to left respectively are the houses of Moorside and Strinesdale, now named Pennine Meadows, with Watersheddings beyond. Off picture at the top is the town centre, to the left are the Saddleworth villages and to the right is Shaw. *(Oldham Evening Chronicle)*

BELOW: Photographed in the mid-1960s on Delph Road at Grains Bar while on test following repairs is Roe-bodied Leyland PD2/30 No 433. Off-picture to the left is the junction with the A672 road on which two cars may be seen travelling down towards Denshaw (centre right) The signpost (left) reads "Lancashire" which means that the bus is only just in the then West Riding of Yorkshire and the picture captures the atmosphere of a rural spot at high altitude. *(J. J. Holmes)*

To the supreme summit

The highest point of all Oldham's bus routes was Grains Bar, 1115ft. When service 6 began to operate from Chadderton Hall Park to Denshaw in 1963, the nett vertical rise from Chadderton was 740ft or 123ft/mile with steeper intermediate sections. It was work against the collar for most of the way to Grains Bar and required the full engine power. Tables 3a/b give the relevant figures.

Table 3a
Service 6: Chadderton Hall Park - Denshaw

Route locations	Time allowed (mins)	Miles from start	Altitude (feet)	Remarks
Chadderton Hall Park	-	-	375	Expensive residential area with open spaces.
Burnley La/Broadway	-	0.6	450	Moderate climbing so far.
Westhulme Av	07	1.3	525	Older properties, heavily populated.
Chadderton Rd/Featherstall Rd	-	1.6	565	Some industry. Steeper gradients ahead.
Barker St (summit)	-	2.1	700	Practically continuous climb from start.
Market Place	12	2.4	691	Busy interchange. Main shopping area.
Mumps Bridge	-	3.0	594	Gradual descent from Barker St.
Huddersfield Rd/Ripponden Rd	-	3.6	679	Steady climb through industrial/residential area.
Watersheddings	-	4.1	820	Less industry. Becoming more open.
Moorside	25	4.9	892	Views to distant Irwell Valley and Winter Hill, left. Much open country, Moorside - Denshaw.
Grains Bar	30	6.0	1115	Exposed summit. Highest point on bus system.
Nr Golden Fleece	-	6.9	954	Hazardous S-bend with unsighted junction. Land falls steeply to right. Magnificent vista across Upper Tame Valley to Standedge.
Denshaw	35	7.5	890	Sheltered village on trans-Pennine turnpike route.

Table 3b
Examples of height gained and lost over distance, service 6

Locations	Height gained or lost (ft)	Distance (miles)	Ft/mile basis	Remarks
Chadderton Hall Park - Barker St (summit)	+325	2.1	+155	
Chadd Rd/F'stall Rd - Barker St (summit)	+135	0.5	+270	Barker St later overbuilt
Chadderton Hall Park - Grains Bar	+740	6.0	+123	
Mumps Bridge - Grains Bar	+521	3.0	+174	Arduous climb after first 0.6m .
Huddersfield Rd/Ripponden Rd - Grains Bar	+436	2.4	+182	Frequent changes of gradient.
Grains Bar - Denshaw	−225	1.5	−150	

BELOW: Hardly "Terrain" but definitely an operating hazard! Pennine bodied No 115 passing under the low bridge in Grimshaw Lane at Middleton Junction Station shortly after being absorbed into the SELNEC Southern fleet where it became 5015. *(Ian N. Lynas)*

Big job for small buses

The C service climbed from Middleton Junction to Strinesdale during 1950-57 and was known locally as the "little C" as it was single deck-operated due to low bridges at Middleton Junction and Lansdowne Road. At that time the vehicles were 32-seat Crossleys, relatively small by some later standards. The route was another that placed heavy demands vehicles and drivers as tables 4a/b show. Growlings and whinings from Crossley engines and gearboxes resounded along much of the course.

Table 4a
Service C: Middleton Junction - Strinesdale

Route locations	Time allowed (mins)	Miles from start	Altitude (feet)	Remarks
Middleton Junction	-	-	340	Old industrial and residential area.
Foxdenton La/Broadway	-	1.1	367	Mainly residential. Some industry nearby.
Denton La/Peel St	-	2.2	450	Populous area with industry.
Middleton Rd/Main Rd	-	2.7	496	Older housing. Heavy industry. Steep climb ahead.
Middleton Rd/Westbourne St	-	3.0	551	Densely-populated.
West St/Rochdale Rd	-	3.3	650	Entering central area.
Market Place	15	3.5	691	Busy interchange. Main shopping area.
Mumps Bridge	-	4.1	594	Descent from Market Place.
Huddersfield Rd/Ripponden Rd	-	4.7	679	Steady climb through industrial/residential area.
Watersheddings	-	5.2	820	Less industry. Open land in view soon.
Moorside	27	6.0	892	Steeper climbing ahead.
Strinesdale	31	6.7	1000	Windswept and isolated housing area.

Table 4b
Examples of height gained and lost over distance, service C

Locations	Height gained or lost (ft)	Distance (miles)	Ft/mile basis	Remarks
Middleton Junction - Market Place	+351	3.5	+100	Easy climbing to Middleton Rd
Middleton Rd/Main Rd - Market Place	+195	0.8	+245	Stiff ascent.
Middleton Junction - Strinesdale	+660	6.7	+99	
Mumps Bridge - Strinesdale	+406	2.6	+156	Moderate climbing for first 0.6m.
Huddersfield Rd/Ripponden Rd - Strinesdale	+321	2.0	+160	

BELOW: A grey day on Chamber Road sees Roe-bodied Leyland PD1/3 No 272 pulling hard up the steepest part of Chamber Road, 1 in 9, while a solitary passenger waits at Frederick Street stop in the late 1960's. *(J. J. Holmes)*

Table 1   Fleet Summary

Notes. Engines of same make as chassis except where remarked otherwise. All bodies to 1964 timber-framed except where remarked otherwise; steel-framed from 1965.
In "year withdrawn" column, PTE=to SELNEC PTE 1 Nov 69.
Fleet numbers. A dash between numbers denotes *"to"* (eg, 63-66 means Nos 63 *to* 66). An oblique denotes *"and"* (eg, 63/66 means Nos 63 *and* 66). For clarity, a comma may be used to separate different series of numbers. An oblique in a chassis designation (eg, Leyland PD1/3) is the manufacturer's means of distinguishing variations of design. The function of an oblique in a bodywork code is explained below.
Bodywork descriptive code. This is an unofficial designation giving type of body, seating capacity and entrance position (eg, B32F or H30/26R), explained as follows:
Prefixes: B=single deck bus. **C**=coach. **FB**=fully-fronted single deck bus. **H**=highbridge double deck bus. **L**=lowbridge double deck bus. **O**=open-top double deck bus.
Figures denote seating capacity. An *oblique* indicates upper/lower saloon seating split on double deckers, eg, 30/26 (upper/lower). A *plus* sign (+) precedes the number of standees.
Suffixes: C=centre entrance platform. **D**=dual doorway. **F**=front or forward entrance platform. **R**=rear entrance platform. **RO**=open rear entrance platform and staircase.
Unladen Weight: Pre-metric values are used here. As many readers may be unfamiliar with now forgotten terminology, the abbreviations t. c. and q refer to tons, hundredweight (cwt) and quarters.
(One cwt was equal to 112 pounds (lbs) or one twentieth of a ton (2240 lbs) and a quarter was one quarter of a cwt.)

Trolleybuses

Year	Fleet No(s)	Reg No(s)	Chassis make & type	Motor	Body make & descriptive code	Unladen weight (t.c.q)	Year withdrawn.	Remarks
1925	1/2	BU 3861/3854	Railless	-	Short Bros B36C	-	1926	Fitted with 2x35hp English Electric motors and foot-operated controller.

Motor buses

Year	Fleet No(s)	Reg No(s)	Chassis make & type	Engine sw vol (litres)	Body make & descriptive code	Unladen weight (t.c.q)	Year withdrawn	Remarks
Two-axle model, petrol-electric transmission, four-cylinder engine, 1913								
1913	-	BU 401/402, 11	Tilling-Stevens TTA2	3.464	Tilling-Stevens O18/16RO	-	Note →	BU 11, 402 withdrawn 1917. BU 401 rebodied as single decker 1917. Later altered to run on town gas. Withdrawn 1918. See text.
Two-axle model, battery-powered, 1918								
1918		BU 69	Electromobile	-	Not known	-	1919	Chassis only purchased. Received single deck body from BU 401.
Two-axle models, four-cylinder petrol-engines, 1924-26								
1924	1-5	BU 3402-3406	Leyland C9	6.6	Leyland B24F	4.0.0	1930-34	
1925	6-9	BU 3672-3675	Leyland C7	6.6	Leyland B28F	4.0.0	1932-34	UW may not be correct.
1925	10	TB 2553	Leyland	-	-?- Open-top	-	1925	
1926	10-17	BU 3991-3998	AEC 507	6.787	Roe H26/26RO	5.14.0	1933	Ex-Belgrave Mills, Oldham. Chassis type, body details and year new not known.
Three-axle models, six-cylinder petrol-engines, 1926-28								
1926	18-20	BU 4509-4511	Guy BX	5.76	Roe H26/24RO	6.4.0	1935	Daimler engine.
1926/27	21-27	BU 4574-4580	Guy BKX	5.76	Guy B32F	5.6.2	1934	Daimler engine.
1927	28/29	BU 4838/4839	Karrier WL6/1	6.597	Short Bros B39R	6.9.0	1933	
1927	30-32	BU 4840-4842	Guy FCX	6.796	Roe B39R	5.16.3	1935	Altered to 37 seats, 1931. No31 became driver-training bus, 1935.
1927	33/34	BU 4843/4844	Guy FCX	6.796	Roe H30/26RO	6.10.1	1935	
1928	35	BU 5172	Karrier DD6/1	8.99	Hall, Lewis H36/34R	7.10.0	1933	
1928	36	BU 5173	Guy FCX	7.672	Short Bros H38/34R	6.16.3	1935	
1928	37/38	BU 5264/5262	Karrier CL6	5.945	Hall, Lewis B33R	4.18.0	1933	Dorman engine. Some sources state 34 seats. OCPT records ambiguous.
	39/40	5267/5263						
	41/42	5266/5265						
Two-axle model, four-cylinder petrol engines, ex-J R Tognarelli, Bolton, 1929								
1928	43-48	BU 5550-5555	Karrier DD6	7.79	English Electric H36/30R	7.6.3	1933	
1928	49-56	BU 5556-5563	Guy FCX	7.672	English Electric H36/30R	6.15.3	1936	
1929	57	WH 1352	ADC 426	5.1	Bell B32D	5.11.2	1934	AEC engine. Believed new 1928.
1929	58	WH 1441	ADC 426	5.1	Burlingham B32D	5.11.2	1934	AEC engine. Believed new 1929. One source states 58 had Bell body.
Two-axle models, six-cylinder petrol engines, 1931-32								
1931	59-62	BU 6760-6763	Leyland Tiger TS3	6.8	Roe B31F	5.16.3	1948	Some sources state perimeter seats fitted during WW2 but this not confirmed by OCPT records.
1932	63-66	BU 7102-7105	Leyland Tiger TS4	6.8	Roe B33F	6.2.1	1948	63/66 altered to 30 perimeter seats + 30 standing, 1942/43. 63/65 ran on producer gas between 1942-44.
1932	67	BU 7106	Leyland Tiger TS4	6.8	Shearing & Crabtree B31F	6.2.2	1948	
1932	68-75	BU 7107-7114	Leyland Titan TD2	7.6	Leyland H27/24R	6.13.0	1947/49	72 fitted with Leyland 8.1-litre diesel, Jan 33.
Two-axle models, six-cylinder diesel engines (except where remarked otherwise), 1933-69								
1933	10-17	BU 7600-7607	Leyland Titan TD2	8.1	English Electric H28/26R	6.7.3	1947/48	
1933	21-29	BU 7608-7616	Leyland Tiger TS4	8.1	Roe B32F	5.19.3	1948/50	24 ran on town gas for an unspecified period, 1941. All altered to 30 perimeter seats + 30 standing, 1942/43.
1934	57	BU 7945	Crossley Mancunian	9.12	Roe H29/24R	6.9.2	1949	Altered to 30/26 by 1936.
1934	58	BU 7946	Leyland Titan TD3	8.6	English Electric H28/26R	6.6.3	1948	
1934	18-20	BU 8254-8256	Leyland Tiger TS6	8.6	Roe FB32F	5.19.1	1948	33/35: UW 6.9.0 and 29/24 seats by 1936.
1934	30-35	BU 8257-8262	Leyland Titan TD3	8.6	Roe H30/24R	6.8.0	1947	4: UW 6.10.2. and 28/24 seats when new; to 28/26 by 1937. Others to 30/26 by 1936.
1935	1-5	BU 8421-8425	Crossley Mancunian	9.12	Roe H29/24R	6.9.1	1950	

Year	Fleet No(s)	Reg No(s)	Chassis make & type	Engine sw vol (litres)	Body make & descriptive code	Unladen weight (t.c.q)	Year withdrawn	Remarks
1935	76-101	BU 8426-8451	Leyland Titan TD3	8.6	Roe H30/24R	6.8.0	1947-50	All to 30/26 seats by 1936. 80 ran on producer gas between 1942-44.
1935	102-104	BU 8573-8575	Leyland Titan TD4	8.6	Leyland H26/26R	6.6.1	1954	Metal-framed body.
1936	105	BU 8860	Leyland Titan TD4	8.6	Metro-Cammell H30/26R	6.10.0	1950	Metal-framed body.
1935	106-109	BU 8861-8864	Leyland Titan TD4	8.6	English Electric H30/26R	6.10.0	1948-50	
1935	110-113	BU 8865-8868	Leyland Titan TD4	8.6	Roe H30/26R	6.9.0	1948-50	
1935	114/115	BU 8972/8973	Leyland Titan TD4	8.6	Roe H30/26R	6.10.0	1950/48	
1936	116	BU 8974	Leyland Titan TD4	8.6	Roe H30/26R	6.10.0	1950	Metal-framed body.
1935	117-119	BU 8975-8977	Leyland Titan TD4	8.6	English Electric H30/26R	6.10.0	1948/49	
1936	36-41	BU 9260-9265	Leyland Titan TD4	8.6	English Electric H30/26R	6.10.0	'47/49/50	
1936	42-47	BU 9266-9632	Leyland Titan TD4	8.6	English Electric H30/26R	6.10.0	'49/50/52	
1936	121-125	BU 9621-9626	Leyland Titan TD4	8.6	English Electric H30/26R	6.12.0	1949/50	
1936	126-131	BU 9627-9632	Leyland Titan TD4	8.6	English Electric H30/26R	6.14.0	1957	128 ran on producer gas between 1942-44.
1937	132-152	ABU 350-370	Leyland Titan TD5	8.6	English Electric H30/26R	6.13.0	'48/52/54	
1937	153-167	ABU 371-385	Leyland Titan TD5	8.6	Roe H31/25R	6.14.2	1955-57	These and future Roe bodies to 1958 fitted with "safety staircase".
1937	168-173	ABU 386-391	Daimler COG6	8.4	Roe H28/25R	6.18.3	1955/57	Gardner engine
1938	174-179	ABU 859-864	Leyland Titan TD5	8.6	Leyland H30/26R	6.11.2	1956/57	Metal-framed body.
1939-41	180-226	CBU 180-226	Leyland Titan TD5	8.6	Roe H31/25R	6.14.2	1957/58	205 converted to breakdown tender 1958, scrapped 1968. Ex-Yelloway Motor Services, Rochdale; new 1938. Metal-framed body.
1944	227	DDK 256	Leyland Tiger TS1	6.8	Burlingham C29R	6.13.3	1952	Ex-Yelloway; new 1931; petrol-engined. Not operated.
1944	-	DK 7378/7379	Leyland Titan PD1	7.4	Roe H31/25R	7.2.2	1944	Not operated.
1946	228-241	DBU 20-33	Leyland Titan PD1/3	7.4	Roe H31/25R	7.9.0	1966/67	
1947	242-266	DBU 242-266	Leyland Titan PD1/3	7.4	Roe H31/25R	7.9.0	↑	*These and future OCPT buses to 1969, 8ft wide.* 246 to PTE, SELNEC No5246 (not applied); preserved. Others withdrawn 1966/67.
1948	267-291	DBU 267-291	Leyland Titan PD1/3	7.4	Roe H31/25R		1966/68	
1948	292-301	DBU 292-301	Crossley SD42/3	8.6	Roe B32F	6.7.3	1961/63/64/66/68	299 fitted with 1951 Crossley metal-framed B32F body ex-Southport Corporation Crossley SD42/7 117, 1965.
1948	302-311	EBU 465-474	Crossley DD42/5	8.6	Crossley H30/26R	8.0.2	1963/65	Metal-framed body.
1948	312-321	EBU 912-921	Daimler CVD6	8.6	Crossley H31/25R	7.19.2	1965/66	Metal-framed body.
1949	322-336	EBU 922-936	Daimler CVD6	8.6	Crossley H30/26R	8.1.0	1966	
1948	337	EBU 867	Leyland Titan PD2/3	9.8	Crossley H31/25R	7.18.1	1966	
1950	338-351	EBU 868-881	Leyland Titan PD2/3	9.8	Roe H31/25R	7.17.3	↑	*This column: four-figure numbers are those of SELNEC, introduced 1970* 341/342/345/349/360 to PTE, 5241 etc (some not applied). Others withdrawn 1968/69.
1950	352-361	FBU 639-648	Crossley SD42/7	8.6	Roe B32F	6.11.2	1965-67	
1950	366-369	FBU 825-828	Crossley DD42/8	8.6	Crossley H30/26R	8.0.1	1966-68	Metal-framed body. 368 preserved.
1952	370-372	HBU 123-125	Titan PD2/12 *(This column: Leyland)*	9.8	Leyland H30/26R	7.17.3	↑	Metal-framed body. These and future buses to 1958 27ft long. 370 to PTE; not renumbered. Others withdrawn 1968.
1955	373-377	KBU 383-387	Titan PD2/20	9.8	Metro-Cammell H30/26R	7.0.2	PTE	Metal-framed body. 5273 etc. Some withdrawn before renumbering.
1954	378-387	KBU 373-382	Titan PD2/20	9.8	Roe H31/25R	7.16.1	PTE	5278 etc.
1957	388-407	NBU 488-507	Titan PD2/20	9.8	Roe H33/27R	7.13.0	PTE	Aluminium alloy-framed upper saloon. 5288 etc. 394 preserved.
1957	408-412	NBU 508-512	Titan PD2/20	9.8	Crossley H33/28R	7.9.2	PTE	Metal-framed body. Only 409 operated by PTE; 5309.
1957	413-418	NBU 513-518	Titan PD2/20	9.8	NCME H33/28R	7.12.1	PTE	Metal-framed body. 5313 etc.
1958/59	419-428	PBU 919-928	Titan PD2/30	9.8	Metro-Cammell 37/28R	7.14.2	PTE	Metal-framed body. 5319 etc.
1958	429-452	PBU 929-952	Titan PD2/30	9.8	Roe H37/28R	7.16.2	PTE	Aluminium alloy-framed upper saloon. 5329 etc.
1958/59	453-462	PBU 953-962	Titan PD2/30	9.8	NCME H37/28R	7.12.1	PTE	Metal-framed body. 5353 etc. Others: 5354 etc.
1958/59	101-110	101-110 HBU	Titan PD3/5	9.8	Roe H41/32F	8.13.2	↑	These and future Atlanteans 30ft long. 108 withdrawn 1968 following collision. Others to PTE, 5101 etc. Aluminium alloy-framed upper saloon
1964	111-114	111-114 JBU	Tiger Cub PSUC1/13	6.54	Marshall B41D	6.14.3	PTE	5011 etc.
1964	115/116	115/116 JBU	Tiger Cub PSUC1/13	6.54	Pennine B41D	7.4.1	PTE	5015 etc.
1965	121-130	CBU 121-130C	Atlantean PDR1/1 MkII	9.8	Roe H43/34F	8.16.2	PTE	5121 etc.
1965	463	LWE 104	Titan PD2/1	9.8	Leyland H30/26R	7.10.2		463-466: ex-Sheffield Trans Dept. New 1949. 463 withdrawn before SELNEC renumbering. Others: 5364 etc, but not necessarily applied.
1965	464-466	LWE 109-111	Titan PD2/1	9.8	Leyland H30/26R	7.10.2	1968	
1965	467-470	ACP 392/385/388/390	Titan PD2/1	9.8	Leyland H33/26R	7.10.2	PTE	Ex-Halifax Corp. 467 new 1948, others 1947. 470 was to have been converted to breakdown tender following withdrawal but conversion never completed.
1965	471-474	DBN 329/330/337/342	Titan PD2/4	9.8	Leyland H32/26R	7.10.2	PTE	Ex-Bolton Corp, new 1949. 5471 etc but 5372-5374 not applied.
1966	131-135	GBU 131-135D	Atlantean PDR1/1 MkII	9.8	East Lancs H43/34F	8.16.0	PTE	5131 etc.
1966	136-147	GBU 136-147D	Atlantean PDR1/1 MkII	9.8	Roe H43/34F	8.16.2	PTE	5136 etc.
1966	475-478	OWB 856/857/859/861	Titan PD2/10	9.8	Leyland H33/28R	7.13.0	PTE	Ex-Sheffield Trans Dept, new 1952. 5475 etc. 5478 not applied.
1967	148-152	LBU 148-152E	Atlantean PDR1/1 MkII	9.8	Neepsend H43/34F	8.16.2	PTE	5148 etc.
1967	153-160	LBU 153-160E	Atlantean PDR1/1 MkII	9.8	Roe H43/34F	8.16.2	PTE	5153 etc.
1967	117-120	LBU 117-120E	Panther Cub PSRC1/1	6.54	Marshall B45D	7.14.2	PTE	33ft 6in long. 5017 etc.
1967/68	161-171	OBU 161-171F	Atlantean PDR1/1 MkII	11.1	Roe H43/34F	8.17.0	PTE	5161 etc. 163 preserved.
1969	172-177	SBU 172-177F	Panther PSUR1/1	11.1	Marshall B48+20D	8.17.0	PTE	36ft long. 5022 etc.
1970	178-182	SBU 178-182F	Atlantean PDR1A/1	11.1	Roe H43/31D	9.4.3	PTE	5178 etc.
1971	183-187	WBU 183-187H	Atlantean PDR1A/1	11.1	Roe H43/31D	9.5.3	-	Ordered by OCPT but delivered to SELNEC as 5183 etc in OCPT livery. These and 5188-5199 8ft 2½in wide.
	188-199	ABU 188-199J	Atlantean PDR1A/1	11.1	Roe H43/34D	9.5.3	-	Ordered by OCPT but delivered to SELNEC in PTE livery.

101

Table 2   Withdrawal of Oldham Corporation buses by PTE

Note. To 31 Mar 74: SELNEC. From 1 Apr 74: Greater Manchester Original fleet numbers given

Year	Fleet numbers
1970	246, 341/342/345/349/360, 370, 373-376, 408/410-412, 453, 463/464/466, 473/474.
1971	377, 419/420/423/425, 435/450, 454-456/460.
1972	445.
1973	378-387, 409, 418/421/422, 449/452, 457/462.
1974	117/119, 172/175/177, 390/399*/400*, 413*/416*/417, 441*/442*/444*/446*, 459/461*.
1975	112, 173/174/176, 398/400/401, 414, 424/427, 431-434, 437-439/443.
1977	101-107/109/110, 111, 113/114, 436.
1978	115/116, 121-130.
1979	131-135.
1980	136-147, 148-151, 153-160, 167/169-171.
1981	152, 161-166/168, 178/181, 5183/5187.
1982	179/180/182, 5184-5186, 5188-5190/5195/5198.
1983	5191-5193/5196/5197/5199.
1984	5194.

*Did not pass to GM PTE

To GM PTE driver training school at various times 1974-77:   390/391/394**, 414/415(?), 432/433.
To GM PTE apprentice school 1974/75, then sold 1975: 430/438/439
**394 subsequently to GM Museum of Transport for preservation.

Other Oldham Corporation buses *known* to exist, early 1995:
69	(BU 7108)	Leyland TD2	on farm land, Cheshire, in badly deteriorated condition
149	(LBU 149E)	Leyland Atlantean	Manchester Leisure Services (play bus)

Other Oldham Corporation buses that *possibly* exist, early 1995:
127	(CBU 127C)	Leyland Atlantean	Used as caravan in Irish Republic
104	(104 HBU)	Leyland PD3/5	Inverarity Farm, Liff, Tayside (workers' transport)
159	(LBU 159E)	Leyland Atlantean	Stewart (Farmer), Glencarse, Tayside (workers' transport)
160	(LBU 160E)	Leyland Atlantean	Used as store at Pennyburn, N Ireland

Table 3   Buses hired-out during World War 2

Note. 1-4: Crossley Mancunian.   10-17, 68-75: Leyland TD2.   30-35: Leyland TD3.

To Red & White Motor Services, Chepstow

Oldham fleet No	Date returned	Remarks
From 3 Jul 40		
10	11 Dec 44	-
12	8 Dec 44	-
14	25 Jun 44	-
16	15 Oct 45	-
30	30 Oct 45	-
32	31 May 42	-
34	2 Dec 44	-

To Bristol Tramways & Carriage Co

Oldham fleet No	Date returned	Remarks
All from 1 Nov 40		
1	18 Nov 42	-
2	"	Damaged in air raid, 16 Mar 41; repaired.
3	"	Damaged in air raid, 16 Mar 41; repaired.
4	"	-
68	30 Nov 45	BTCC No3723
69	"	BTCC No3724

To Lancashire United Transport & Power Co, Atherton

Oldham fleet No	Date returned	Remarks
From 10 Jun 42		
32	2 Aug 44	-
33	"	-
From 17 Jul 42		
70	15 Jul 46	-
74	"	-

Oldham fleet No	Date returned	Remarks
From 31 Jul 40		
11	31 May 42	-
13	30 Nov 44	-
15	4 Dec 44	-
17	6 Mar 46	-
31	19 Nov 45	-
33	31 May 42	-
35	22 Oct 45	-
70	7 Jul 42	-
71	3 Oct 45	BTCC No3725
72	17 Sep 45	BTCC No3726
73	"	BTCC No3727
74	7 Jul 42	-
75	"	Damaged in air raid, 16 Mar 41; repaired
75		-

Oldham fleet No	Date returned	Remarks
From 18 Jul 42		
75		-

Table 4   Buses hired-in—1965

From (Lending operator)	Fleet number(s)	Registration numbers(s)	Chassis	Body	Year new	Remarks
Bolton Corporation	400	CWH 750	Leyland Titan PD2/4	Leyland H32/26R	1949	
	401/426*/427*/434*/438	DBN 304/329/330/337/341	"	"	1949	*Subsequently acquired, plus 439 (DBN 342)
Bradford Corporation	207-209	6207-6209 KW	AEC Regent V LD3RA	Metro-Cammell H40/30F	1964	30ft long
Bury Corporation	158/159	EN 9958/9959	Leyland Titan PD2/3	Weymann H30/2R	1949	
Manchester Corporation	3175/3176/3199	JNA 476/477/500	Leyland Titan PD1/3	Metro-Cammell H32/26R	1949/50	
	3266/3267/3270/3276/ 3277/3280/3281	JND 667/668/671/677/ JND 678/681/68	Leyland Titan PD2/3	Leyland H32/26R	1950	
Rochdale Corporation	227-229, 233	HDK 27-29, 833	AEC Regent III 9612E	Weymann H33/26R	1949, 1951	
St Helens Corporation	E74/E76/E80	CDJ 719/721/880	Leyland Titan PD2/10	Davies H30/26R	1954	
Salford Corporation	407-412	CRJ 407-412	Daimler CVG6	Metro-Cammell H30/24R	1950	
Sheffield Transport Dept	832-836	YWA 832/836	Leyland Titan PD2/20	Roe H33/25R	1957	
Stockport Corporation	24/25	BJA 924/925B	Leyland Titan PD2/40	East Lancs H36/28R	1964	
Wigan Corporation	25/27	JP 6018/6028	Leyland Titan PD1	Leyland L27/26R	1947	
	32, 163	JP 8317, 8326	Leyland Titan PD2/1	Leyland H30/26R	1950	

Appendix 4
Summary of Statistical Information

Notes. Some columns include tram figures in brackets for comparison. All working expenses include cost of fuels. Most figures rounded for clarity.

1	2	3	4	5	6	7	8	9	10	11	12
Year ending 31 Mar	Bus miles operated × 1,000	Passgrs carried × 1,000	Average passgrs per bus mile	Bus (tram) traffic revenue £ × 1,000	Bus (tram) working expenses £ × 1,000	Traf rev per bus mile [old pence]	W exps per bus mile [old pence]	W exps as proportion of receipts	Buses in stock	Nett surplus or deficit (−) £	Remarks
1914	29	305	10.5	1,325 (114)	1,617 (78)	11.0d	13.4d	122%	3	−306	Operations from May 1913. Col 5 gives total bus revenue for 1913-14.
1915	32	290	9.1	1,302 (112)	1,801 (85)	10.2d	13.6d	133%	3	−1,015	
1916	27	248	9.2	1,193 (118)	1,351 (82)	10.7d	12.0d	112%	3	−718	Reduced service from Aug 1916
1917	20	229	11.5	1,047 (125)	1,591 (85)	12.9d	19.9d	148%	3	−1,084	
1918	13	154	12.0	0.595 (149)	1,508 (107)	11.2d	28.0d	252%	1	−1,117	
1919	15	120	7.8	0.713 (182)	1,627 (124)	11.2d	25.4d	227%	2	−915	Service ended Sep 1919
1920	7	61	8.3	0.387 (235)	1,452 (169)	14.8d	48.0d	324%	2	−1,003	
(Cols 2 & 3 in millions from 1925)											
1925	0.28	1.87	-	13 (227)	12 (192)	11.0d	10.7d	-	5	−1,470	Only 3 months' operations
1926	0.68	5.82	6.7	42 (218)	34 (196)	14.9d	12.0d	97%	15	1,931	
1927	1.01	7.08	8.5	52 (221)	49 (189)	12.9d	11.6d	80%	22	−3,131	
1928	1.40	9.80	7.0	77 (206)	71 (168)	13.2d	12.2d	90%	42	−5,319	
1929	1.78	13.6	7.0	105 (192)	104 (156)	14.2d	14.1d	90%	56	−20,073	
1930	1.68	12.2	7.7	101 (176)	89 (143)	14.4d	12.7d	99%	58	−8,847	
1931	1.65	12.2	7.3	100 (171)	82 (137)	14.5d	11.9d	88%	56	−3,209	
1932	1.67	12.7	7.5	99 (157)	74 (131)	14.3d	10.7d	82%	63	9,950	
1933	1.76	13.9	7.7	109 (153)	76 (129)	14.8d	11.3d	75%	70	12,455	
1934	1.77	14.9	7.9	110 (154)	83 (126)	14.9d	11.3d	70%	53	11,358	
1935	2.75	24.4	8.5	164 (110)	114 (103)	14.3d	9.9d	75%	90	22,007	
1936	3.35	31.8	9.2	201 (84)	137 (79)	14.1d	9.8d	69%	101	26,271	Tramway replacement programme begun
1937	3.89	38.3	9.5	235 (73)	176 (69)	14.5d	10.9d	68%	118	18,046	Best-ever figure in Col 9.
1938	4.53	44.3	10.1	n/a	n/a	14.0d	11.4d	75%	166	18,802	No further tram figures available.
1939			9.8					n/a	166		Some wartime and later bus figures not available.
1940	3.98	43.7	10.8	308	n/a	18.6d	12.7d	n/a	213	16,593	Col 2 figures for 1940-43 extrapolated from totals including trams.
1941	3.49	45.2	12.6	325	n/a	19.1d	15.5d	n/a	213	31,867	
1942	3.56	49.9	14.0	366	n/a	21.2d	17.2d	n/a	213	33,248	
1943	3.49	52.0	14.9	388	n/a	22.8d	18.5d	n/a	213	9,265	
1944	3.30	50.3	15.2	375	308	23.4d	19.7d	n/a	214	8,940	Highest-ever passengers per mile.
1945	3.46	51.6	14.9	401	321	24.4d	19.9d	82%	214	34,757	
1946	3.74	52.6	14.1	421	345	23.8d	19.8d	84%	214	22,327	
1947	4.67	64.6	13.8	470	395	23.2d	19.4d	84%	228	31,826	Completion of tramway replacement during year.
1948	5.19	71.6	13.8	521	438	24.1d	18.2d	85%	228	51,452	First full year of bus-only operation. Highest-ever surplus.
1949	5.57	76.3	13.7	559	475	24.1d	18.7d	86%	236	42,831	
1950	5.98	80.8	13.5	599	515	24.0d	20.7d	93%	239	18,783	
1951	6.13	81.6	13.3	604	562	23.6d	22.0d	94%	240	−32,348	
1952	5.99	77.6	13.0	665	625	26.2d	25.1d	90%	240	−18,117	
1953	5.97	80.0	13.4	741	667	29.8d	27.0d	92%	240	13,621	
1954	5.98	77.0	12.9	740	680	29.7d	27.3d	92%	240	5,555	
1955	6.07	82.4	13.6	754	n/a	29.8d	n/a	n/a	240	−16,243	
1956	6.13	87.5	14.3	828	n/a	32.4d	n/a	n/a	240	25,131	Highest-ever number of passengers carried.
1957	6.18	79.6	12.9	884	822	34.3d	31.9d	93%	235	13,734	Highest-ever mileage operated.
1958	6.05	76.2	12.6	854	845	33.7d	33.5d	99%	235	−22,006	Passenger totals declining significantly.
1959	6.03	73.6	12.2	876	n/a	34.9d	n/a	n/a	235	−4,619	
1960	6.04	71.7	11.9	914	832	36.3d	33.0d	91%	233	12,819	
1961	5.97	69.7	11.7	948	882	38.1d	35.4d	93%	233	14,364	
1962	5.96	67.8	11.4	993	914	40.0d	36.9d	92%	231	12,770	
1963	5.85	66.8	11.4	1,025	941	41.9d	38.5d	92%	233	19,530	
1964	5.95	66.5	11.2	1,081	999	43.5d	40.2d	92%	233	−8,822	
1965	5.94	64.6	10.9	1,101	1,022	44.5d	41.2d	93%	233	−11,486	
1966	5.92	60.0	10.1	1,209	1,101	49.0d	45.0d	92%	233	−49,249	Highest-ever deficit
1967	5.66	56.5	10.0	1,284	1,156	54.4d	49.2d	90%	233	−38,524	
1968	5.25	51.3	9.8	1,222	1,161	55.9d	53.0d	95%	207	36,753	
1969	5.31	51.0	9.6	1,312	1,264	59.3d	57.1d	96%	200	22,574	Working expenses per mile more than double 1954 figure.

Committee Chairmen and General Managers

Table 1 —Chairmen of the Tramways/Passenger Transport Committee 1898-1969

1898-1901	Alderman J Eckersley		1936-38	Alderman I Crabtree
1901-04	Alderman H Chadwick		1938-46	Alderman A Hallwood
1904-08	Councillor J S Dronsfield		1946-47	Alderman H Holt
1908-10	Alderman S Dunkerley		1947-48	Alderman A Hallwood
1910-11	Councillor F G Isherwood		1948-52	Councillor A Hallwood
1911-12	Councillor J Middleton		1952-54	Alderman H Holt
1912-13	Councillor F G Isherwood		1954-56	Councillor S T Marron
1913-16	Alderman F G Isherwood		1956-60	Alderman J Brown
1916-26	Councillor J K Cheetham		1960-67	Councillor J Shyne
1926-29	Alderman J K Cheetham		1967-68	Councillor C McCall
1929-36	Councillor I Crabtree		1968-69	Councillor E Leeks

Note : *Reversion to Councillor from Alderman. Oldham had a system of appointing Aldermen for a period of six years, or multiples of six. In some circumstances they could then revert to Councillor.*

Table 2 — General Managers, 1898-1969

1898-1902	A consulting engineer		1918-25	W Chamberlain*
1902-04	R H Wilkinson		1925-29	C Jackson
1904-11	L Slattery		1929-44	J F Richards
1911-16	J W Dugdale		1944-61	C P Paige
1916-18	P Priestly		1961-69	H Taylor

Later Sir William Chamberlain

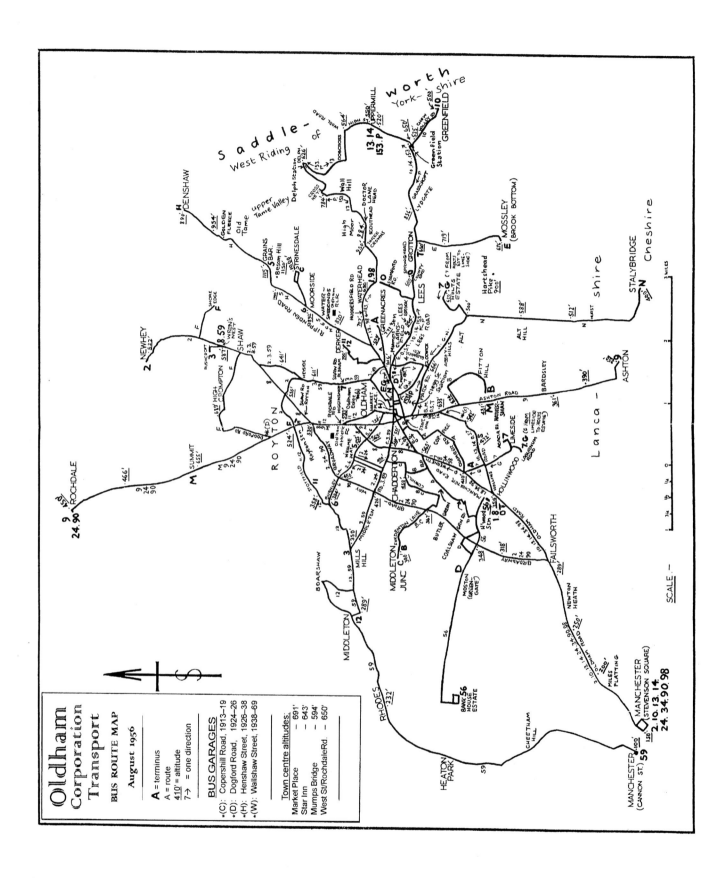

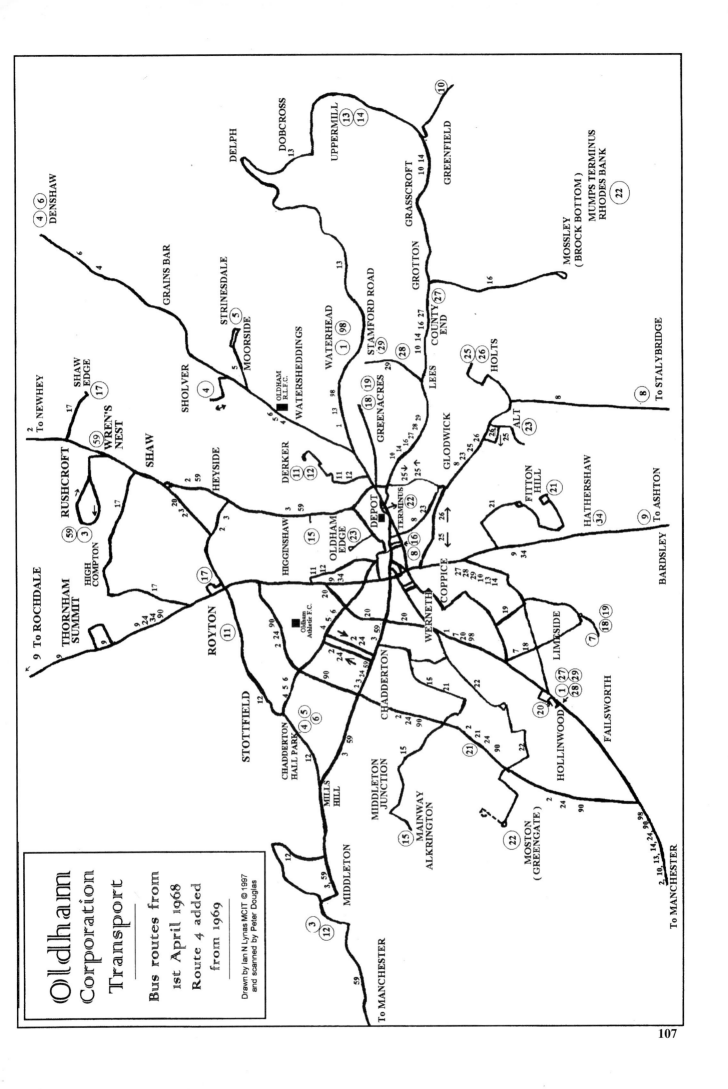

Oldham Corporation Transport

Bus routes from 1st April 1968

Route 4 added from 1969

Drawn by Ian N Lynas MCIT © 1997
and scanned by Peter Douglas

107

Bibliography

Appleby J. B.	*Cheltenham's Trams & Buses Remembered*	TPC 1973
Brown S. J.	*Albion & Crossley Buses in Camera*	Ian Allan 1982
Butterworth E. P.	*Historical Sketches of Oldham*	Morten 1981 (reprint)
Eyre M. & Heaps C.	*The Manchester Bus*	TPC 1989
Hannay R. N.	*Guy Motors and the Wulfrunian*	TPC 1978
Hilditch G. G.	*Looking at Buses*	Ian Allan 1978
Jack D.	*The Leyland Bus*	TPC 1984
Marshall P. J.	*British Bus Fleets: Lancashire*	Ian Allan 1960
Marshall R.	*Chas H Roe, Vol 1*	TPC 1979
Ogden E. & Hyde W. G. S.	*SHMD Joint Board*	TPC 1990
Pettie J.	*Guy Buses in Camera*	Ian Allan 1979
Townsin A. A.	*The Best of British Buses* series:	TPC 1981-86
	Leyland Tigers 1927-81	
	Leyland Titans 1927-42	
	Leyland Titans 1945-84	
	Post-war Daimlers 1942-81	
	The British Bus Story series:	TPC 1983-85
	A Golden Age - 1946-50	
	A Wind of Change - The 'Fifties	
	Turbulent Times - The 'Sixties	
Smith E. J.	*ABC Buses and Coaches*	Ian Allan 1956
Warburton D. J.	*ABC Buses and Coaches*	Ian Allan 1955
Wild J. M.	*The Oldham Bus Scene, 1945-69*	Wild 1970
Yearsley I. & Groves P.	*The Manchester Tramways*	TPC 1988

Magazines, newspapers, periodicals and journals

Buses Illustrated—later *Buses*
Bus & Coach
Modern Transport
Municipal Passenger Transport Association Journal
Oldham Evening Chronicle
Oldham Tramways/Passenger Transport Committee: minutes of meetings
Oldham Tramways/Passenger Transport Department: annual reports
PSV Circle/Omnibus Society Fleet Histories
Tramway & Railway World—later *Transport World*
Tramway Review

BACK COVER ILLUSTRATIONS—

TOP PICTURE: The Leyland Panthers were well-proportioned, attractive saloons and 177 is seen here on a private hire, meeting a Ribble Leyland PD3 'Sabrina'. *(Photobus—P. Eckersley)*

CENTRE LEFT: Nice and clean—380 and stablemates repose in Wallshaw Street garage. *(Photobus—Arnold Richardson)*

CENTRE RIGHT: Acquired from Sheffield Transport Dept in 1965, 465 looks well in its new livery as it waits at the West St/Rochdale Rd junction with the Civic Centre perimeter wall on the right and the college in the background *(Photobus—Arnold Richardson)*

LOWER RIGHT: Captured here as SELNEC 5317 with black Helvetica numerals, 414 nears the end of its limited stop run from Manchester to Uppermill as it ambles down the Upper Tame Valley between Delph and Dobcross with Knott Hill dominating the skyline. *(Photobus—Arnold Richardson)*

The Author

The author, who has been fascinated by buses and trams from an early age during World War 2, is a committed enthusiast for public transport and believes that a stable and integrated network can be created and sustained only by radical and co-ordinated policies. Concerned for the preservation of the past as well as for the securing of the future of public transport he is actively involved in several preservation societies; drives preserved trams at the Heaton Park Tramway, Manchester, in a voluntary capacity; is a member of the Greater Manchester Transportation Consultative Committee and its Buses Sub-Committee, and of the Greater Manchester Passenger Transport Authority Oldham Local Transport Group; and founder and convener of Oldham Transport Users' Forum. For many years he has driven buses and coaches on a casual basis for a former National Bus Company operator, and his other interests lie in poetry, music and writing transport magazine articles. Oh! And when not occupied with these matters, he does a full-time job in local government.

Other books by the same author

Weekend Bus Driver (Sheaf Publishing)
Manchester Area Buses (Sheaf Publishing)
Sunderland Corporation Buses (Northeast Press, due for publication 1997)